WHAT'S COOKING
potatoes

Jenny Stacey

THUNDER BAY
P·R·E·S·S

First published in the United States in 2000 by

Thunder Bay Press
An imprint of the Advantage Publishers Group
5880 Oberlin Drive
San Diego, CA 92121-4794
www.advantagebooksonline.com

Copyright © Dempsey Parr 1998

Library of Congress Cataloging in Publication Data available upon request.

ISBN: 1-57145-251-6

Printed in Indonesia

Produced by Haldane Mason, London

Acknowledgments
Art Director: Ron Samuels
Editorial Director: Sydney Francis
Editorial Consultant: Christopher Fagg
Managing Editor: Jo-Anne Cox
Editor: Felicity Jackson
Design: Digital Artworks Partnership Ltd
Photography: Andrew Sydenham
Home Economist: Kathryn Hawkins

Note
Unless otherwise stated, milk is assumed to be full fat, eggs are medium,
and pepper is freshly ground black pepper.

Contents

Introduction

The potato is one of the world's most popular vegetables, cultivated in almost every country. There are many different varieties, native to these countries, each having a different quality or property. As a result of this, the potato suits most culinary styles and is perhaps the most versatile staple food available. It is recognized as one of the most important crops cultivated for human consumption, with Russia, Poland, and Germany being the highest consumers, closely followed by Holland, Cyprus, and Ireland.

On average we eat 242 pounds per head per annum, which is good news when you consider the nutritional properties of this best-loved tuber. The average 8-ounce potato, containing 180 calories, has protein, starch for energy, and fiber, as well as being a good source of vitamin C. Most of the vitamins are found just beneath the skin, which is why it is often suggested that potatoes are cooked in their skins and then peeled. If not cooked with fat, the potato has a great role to play in the slimming diet, a fact which has been disputed in the past.

However, the potato has not always been held in such high regard. It originated in South America and is thought to date back to as far as 3,000 BC. First known as the *papa* and eaten by the Incas, the potato was unknown to the rest of the world until the sixteenth century when Spanish conquistador Francisco Pizarro captured Peru, which was famed for its richness in minerals. The mineral trade brought many people to Peru, who, in turn, carried the potato to the rest of the world. It was known by many names, which reflected the different cooking methods used by the Indians. Even this far back in its history, the potato was eaten fresh in season, and dried by the Incas for use in the winter. Nowadays the storage life of potatoes and the different methods of preservation have increased its popularity in the food market.

The potato first arrived in Europe via Spain, and its name gradually changed from *papa* to *battata*. It became famous for both its nutritional and healing properties—the Italians believed it could heal a wound if the cooked flesh was rubbed into the infected area. One person in particular who believed this was Pope Pious IV, who was sent the potato when he was ill, and then grew his own crop in Italy. It then spread to Belgium, Germany, Switzerland, and France, but did not reach the British Isles until Frances Drake stopped in the New World and shared his cargo (mainly potatoes) with the starving English colonists.

Later repatriated by Sir Walter Raleigh, the colonists brought the potato to Britain, where Raleigh grew the crop on his land. Raleigh was also responsible for taking the potato to Ireland, discovering that Irish soil was perfect for growing it. The starving Irish soon adopted the potato as their own and it became a mainstay of their diet.

Today there are many varieties of potato, each being suitable for different cooking methods, be it roasting, boiling, steaming, baking, mashing, or frying. What makes it particularly versatile is the fact that it absorbs other flavors very readily and it has a consistency which lends itself to many uses.

CHOOSING AND USING POTATOES

Look for a firm, regular-shaped potato, either red or yellow in color, with a smooth, tight skin. Avoid potatoes which are turning green or sprouting, as the flavor will be bitter and they will have higher levels of the natural toxins called glycoalkaloids. Store potatoes in a cool, dark, dry place, as too much light turns them green.

Waxy potatoes, such as Maris Peer, have a firm texture and do not disintegrate during cooking, making them especially suitable for salads. They are also good boiled in their skins. Mealy potatoes, sometimes called floury potatoes, have softer-textured flesh, so are suitable for boiling and mashing. Examples are King Edwards and Red Pontiacs.

TYPES OF POTATO

There are about 3,000 known varieties of potato, but only about 100 of these are regularly grown. Of these, about 20 are found with ease on our supermarket shelves. The following is a brief description of the most popular varieties and their uses, as a guide for the recipes in this book.

Charlotte New Potatoes

Craig Royal Red: *a maincrop potato, ready in July, it is non-mealy and has a pink or red skin. A waxy potato, it is best for frying and boiling, or using in salads.*

Cyprus New Potato: *found in late winter and spring, it is best simply scrubbed and boiled. Not a good mashing potato.*

Desiree: *a high quality, pink-skinned mealy potato, good for baking, frying, boiling, and mashing.*

Home Guard: *generally the first of the new potatoes. It blackens easily and collapses on cooking, so it is best boiled lightly in its skin.*

Jersey Royal: *a delicious new potato. It appears from May to October, but is at its peak in August. It has a flaky skin and firm yellow flesh.*

King Edward: *a large potato which is creamy white, or sometimes yellow in color. Ideal for all cooking methods, it is a very popular variety.*

Maris Piper: *a medium-firm potato with creamy white flesh. It is good for boiling and frying.*

New Potatoes: *these generally have a white flesh and grow quickly. They are dug up in early summer and are best scraped and boiled to use in salads or eaten with melted butter.*

Pentland Crown: *a thin-skinned, creamy white potato which is at its best in late winter. It has a mealy texture, making it ideal for mashing and baking.*

Pentland Hawk: *a firm, pale potato with pale yellow flesh, it is a general, all-purpose potato.*

Pentland Squire: *a firm, white-fleshed potato, which is suitable for all methods of cooking.*

Pink Fir Apple: *this long, knobby potato has pink flesh and a firm, waxy texture. Good in salads.*

White Sweet Potato: *smaller than the yam, although interchangeable, it is yellow-fleshed with a drier texture. Best fried, boiled, or casseroled, it is ideal with spices.*

Yam: *a red sweet potato which is orange-fleshed. It is best mashed in cakes and soufflés or roasted.*

Francine

Anya

Pentland Squire

Soups & Salads

Potatoes form the basis of many delicious and easy-to-prepare homemade soups, as they are the perfect thickening ingredient while adding a subtle flavor. With the addition of just a few ingredients, you have a whole selection of inexpensive soups at your fingertips. Add herbs, onion, garlic, meat, fish, or vegetables, top with herbs or croûtons, simply serve with crusty bread for anything from a light starter to a filling meal.

Also featured in this chapter are salads based on potatoes. In addition to the creamy potato salads with herbs that are so popular, there are many other recipes to tempt your palate. There are well-known classics as well as innovative alternatives. There are salads suitable for light lunches as well as hearty main-course salads. Many are also ideal for barbecues and picnics.

Sweet Potato & Onion Soup

This simple recipe uses the sweet potato with its distinctive flavor and color as the base for a delicious soup with a hint of orange and cilantro.

Serves 4

INGREDIENTS

2 tbsp vegetable oil
2 pounds sweet potatoes, diced
1 carrot, diced
2 onions, sliced
2 garlic cloves, crushed

$2\frac{1}{2}$ cups vegetable stock
$1\frac{1}{4}$ cups unsweetened orange juice
1 cup unsweetened yogurt
2 tbsp chopped fresh cilantro
salt and pepper

TO GARNISH:
cilantro sprigs
orange rind

1 Heat the vegetable oil in a large saucepan and add the diced sweet potatoes and carrot, sliced onions, and garlic. Sauté gently for 5 minutes, stirring constantly.

2 Add the vegetable stock and orange juice and bring to a boil.

3 Reduce the heat to a simmer, cover the saucepan, and cook the vegetables for 20 minutes or until the sweet potato and carrot cubes are tender.

4 Transfer the mixture to a food processor or blender in batches and process for 1 minute until puréed. Return the purée to the rinsed-out saucepan.

5 Stir in the unsweetened yogurt and chopped cilantro and season to taste. Serve the soup garnished with cilantro sprigs and orange rind.

COOK'S TIP

This soup can be chilled before serving, if preferred. If chilling it, stir the yogurt into the dish just before serving. Serve in chilled bowls.

Potato, Apple, & Arugula Soup

Arugula is a fashionable salad green, which has a slightly bitter flavor. It also gives a delicate green coloring to this soup.

Serves 4

INGREDIENTS

4 tbsp butter
2 pounds waxy potatoes, diced
1 red onion, quartered
1 tbsp lemon juice
4¹/₂ cups chicken stock

1 pound eating apples, peeled and diced
pinch of ground allspice
1³/₄ ounces arugula leaves
salt and pepper

TO GARNISH:
slices of red apple
chopped scallions

1 Melt the butter in a large saucepan and add the diced potatoes and sliced red onion. Sauté gently for 5 minutes, stirring constantly.

2 Add the lemon juice, chicken stock, diced apples, and the ground allspice.

3 Bring to a boil, then reduce the heat to a simmer, cover the pan, and cook for 15 minutes.

4 Add the arugula to the soup and cook for a further 10 minutes, until the potatoes are cooked through.

5 Transfer half the soup to a food processor or blender and process for 1 minute. Return to the pan and stir the purée into the remaining soup.

6 Season to taste with salt and pepper. Ladle into hot soup bowls and garnish with the apple slices and chopped scallions. Serve at once with warm crusty bread.

COOK'S TIP

If arugula is unavailable, use baby spinach instead for a similar flavor.

Indian Potato & Pea Soup

A slightly hot and spicy Indian flavor is given to this soup with the use of garam masala, chili, cumin, and cilantro.

Serves 4

INGREDIENTS

2 tbsp vegetable oil
8 ounces mealy potatoes, diced
1 large onion, chopped
2 garlic cloves, crushed
1 tsp garam masala

1 tsp ground coriander
1 tsp ground cumin
$3^3/4$ cups vegetable stock
1 red chili, chopped
1 cup frozen peas

4 tbsp unsweetened yogurt
salt and pepper
chopped fresh cilantro, to garnish

1 Heat the vegetable oil in a large saucepan and add the diced potatoes, onion, and garlic. Sauté gently for about 5 minutes, stirring constantly.

2 Add the ground spices and cook for 1 minute, stirring all the time.

3 Stir in the vegetable stock and chopped red chili and bring the mixture to a boil. Reduce the heat, cover the pan, and simmer for 20 minutes, until the potatoes begin to break down.

4 Add the peas and cook for a further 5 minutes. Stir in the yogurt and season to taste.

5 Pour into warm soup bowls, garnish with chopped fresh cilantro, and serve hot with warm bread.

COOK'S TIP

Potatoes blend perfectly with spices, this soup being no exception. For an authentic Indian dish, serve this soup with warm nan bread.

VARIATION

For slightly less heat, seed the chili before adding it to the soup. Always wash your hands after handling chilies as they contain volatile oils that can irritate the skin and make your eyes burn if you touch your face.

Broccoli & Potato Soup

*This creamy soup has a delightful pale green coloring and rich
flavor from the blend of tender broccoli and blue cheese.*

Serves 4

INGREDIENTS

2 tbsp olive oil
2 potatoes, diced
1 onion, diced
8 ounces broccoli flowerets

2 cups crumbled blue cheese,
4^1/$_2$ cups vegetable stock
^{2}/$_3$ cup heavy cream
pinch of paprika

salt and pepper

1 Heat the oil in a large
saucepan and add the diced
potatoes and onion. Sauté gently
for 5 minutes, stirring constantly.

2 Reserve a few broccoli
flowerets for the garnish and
add the remaining broccoli to the
pan. Add the cheese and stock.

3 Bring to a boil, then reduce
the heat, cover the pan, and
simmer for 25 minutes, until the
potatoes are tender.

4 Transfer the soup to a food
processor or blender in
2 batches and process until the
mixture is a smooth purée.

5 Return the purée to a clean
saucepan and stir in the cream
and a pinch of paprika. Season to
taste with salt and pepper.

6 Blanch the reserved broccoli
flowerets in a little boiling
water for about 2 minutes, then
drain with a slotted spoon.

7 Pour the soup into warm
bowls and garnish with the
broccoli flowerets and a sprinkling
of paprika. Serve immediately.

COOK'S TIP

*This soup freezes very successfully.
Follow the method described here
up to step 4, and freeze the soup
after it has been puréed. Add
the cream and paprika just before
serving. Garnish and serve.*

Potato & Dried Mushroom Soup

There are many varieties of dried mushrooms available on the market today; although relatively expensive, the concentrated flavor that they add to a dish justifies the cost.

Serves 4

INGREDIENTS

2 tbsp vegetable oil
2 large mealy potatoes, sliced
1 onion, sliced
2 garlic cloves, crushed
4 1/2 cups beef stock
1 ounce dried mushrooms
2 celery stalks, sliced

2 tbsp brandy
salt and pepper

TOPPING:
3 tbsp butter
2 thick slices white bread, crusts
  removed
3 tbsp grated Parmesan cheese

TO GARNISH:
rehydrated dried mushrooms
parsley sprigs

1 Heat the vegetable oil in a large skillet and add the potato and onion slices and the garlic. Sauté gently for 5 minutes, stirring constantly.

2 Add the beef stock, dried mushrooms, and the sliced celery. Bring to a boil, then reduce the heat to a simmer, cover the saucepan, and cook the soup for 20 minutes, until the potatoes are tender.

3 Meanwhile, melt the butter for the topping in the skillet. Sprinkle the bread slices with the grated cheese and fry the slices in the butter for 1 minute on each side, until crisp. Cut each slice into triangles.

4 Stir the brandy into the soup, season with salt and pepper, pour into warm bowls, and top with the triangles. Serve garnished with mushrooms and parsley.

COOK'S TIP

Probably the most popular dried mushroom is the cep, but any variety will add a lovely flavor to this soup. If you do not wish to use dried mushrooms, add 1¾ cups sliced fresh mushrooms of your choice to the soup.

Potato, Split Pea, & Cheese Soup

Split green peas are sweeter than other varieties of split pea
and reduce down to a purée when cooked, which acts as a thickener in soups.

Serves 4

INGREDIENTS

2 tbsp vegetable oil
2 mealy potatoes, diced with skins
   left on
2 onions, diced
1/3 cup split green peas

4 1/2 cups vegetable stock
5 tbsp grated Swiss cheese
salt and pepper

CROUTONS:
3 tbsp butter
1 garlic clove, crushed
1 tbsp chopped fresh parsley
1 thick slice white bread, cubed

---

1 Heat the vegetable oil in a large saucepan and add the diced potatoes and onions. Sauté gently for about 5 minutes, stirring constantly.

2 Add the split green peas to the pan and stir to mix together well.

3 Pour the vegetable stock into the pan and bring to a boil. Reduce the heat to a simmer and cook for 35 minutes, until the potatoes are tender and the split peas cooked.

4 Meanwhile, make the croûtons. Melt the butter in a skillet. Add the garlic, chopped parsley, and bread cubes and cook for about 2 minutes, turning frequently until the bread cubes are golden brown on all sides.

5 Stir the grated cheese into the soup and season to taste with salt and pepper.

6 Pour the soup into warm bowls and sprinkle the croûtons on top. Serve the soup at once.

VARIATION

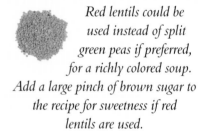

Red lentils could be used instead of split green peas if preferred, for a richly colored soup. Add a large pinch of brown sugar to the recipe for sweetness if red lentils are used.

Leek, Potato, & Bacon Soup

Leek and potato soup is a classic recipe. Here the soup is enhanced with smoked bacon pieces and enriched with heavy cream for a little luxury.

Serves 4

INGREDIENTS

2 tbsp butter
²/₃ cup diced potatoes
4 leeks, shredded
2 garlic cloves, crushed
¹/₂ cup smoked bacon, diced

3³/₄ cups vegetable stock
1 cup heavy cream
2 tbsp chopped fresh parsley
salt and pepper

TO GARNISH:
vegetable oil
1 leek, shredded

1 Melt the butter in a large saucepan and add the diced potatoes, shredded leeks, garlic, and diced bacon. Sauté gently for 5 minutes, stirring constantly.

2 Add the vegetable stock and bring to a boil. Reduce the heat, cover the saucepan, and simmer for 20 minutes, until the potatoes are cooked. Stir in the heavy cream.

3 Meanwhile, make the garnish. Half-fill a pan with oil and heat to 350°F–375°F or until a cube of bread browns in 30 seconds. Add the shredded leek and deep-fry for 1 minute until browned and crisp, taking care as the leek contains water. Drain the leek thoroughly on paper towels and reserve.

4 Reserve a few pieces of potato, leek, and bacon, and set aside. Put the rest of the soup in a food processor or blender in batches and process each batch for 30 seconds. Return the puréed soup to a clean saucepan and heat through.

5 Stir in the reserved vegetables, bacon, and parsley and season to taste. Pour into warm bowls and garnish with the fried leeks.

VARIATION

For a lighter soup, omit the cream and stir yogurt or crème fraîche into the soup at the end of the cooking time.

Potato, Cabbage, & Chorizo Soup

Chorizo is a spicy sausage originating from Spain where it is used to add
its unique strong flavor to enhance many traditional dishes.

Serves 4

INGREDIENTS

2 tbsp olive oil

3 large potatoes, cubed

2 red onions, quartered

1 garlic clove, crushed

4^1/$_2$ cups pork or vegetable stock

1^1/$_2$ cups shredded Savoy cabbage

^{1}/$_2$ cup sliced chorizo sausage

salt and pepper

paprika, to garnish

---

1 Heat the olive oil in a large saucepan and add the cubed potatoes, quartered red onions, and garlic. Sauté gently for 5 minutes, stirring constantly.

2 Add the pork or vegetable stock and bring to a boil. Reduce the heat and cover the saucepan. Simmer the vegetables for about 20 minutes, until the potatoes are tender.

3 Process the soup in a food processor or blender in 2 batches for 1 minute each. Pour the puréed soup into a clean pan.

4 Add the shredded Savoy cabbage and sliced chorizo sausage to the pan and cook for a further 7 minutes. Season to taste.

5 Ladle the soup into warm soup bowls, garnish with a sprinkling of paprika, and serve.

COOK'S TIP

Chorizo sausage requires no pre-cooking. In this recipe, it is added toward the end of the cooking time so that it does not to overpower the other flavors in the soup.

VARIATION

If chorizo sausage is not available, you could use any other spicy sausage or even salami in its place.

Chinese Potato & Pork Broth

In this recipe the pork is seasoned with traditional Chinese flavorings—soy sauce, rice wine vinegar, and a dash of sesame oil.

Serves 4

INGREDIENTS

4¹/₂ cups chicken stock
2 large potatoes, diced
2 tbsp rice wine vinegar
4¹/₂ ounces pork tenderloin, sliced
2 tbsp cornstarch

4 tbsp water
1 tbsp light soy sauce
1 tsp sesame oil
1 carrot, cut into very thin strips
1 tsp fresh ginger root, chopped

3 scallions, sliced thinly
1 red bell pepper, sliced
8 ounce can bamboo shoots, drained

1 Add the stock, diced potatoes, and 1 tbsp of the rice wine vinegar to a saucepan and bring to a boil. Reduce the heat until the stock is just simmering.

2 In a small bowl, mix the cornstarch with the water. Stir the cornstarch mixture into the hot stock.

3 Bring the stock back to a boil, stirring until thickened, then reduce the heat until it is just simmering again.

4 Place the pork slices in a shallow dish and season with the remaining rice wine vinegar, soy sauce, and sesame oil.

5 Add the pork slices, carrot strips, and chopped ginger to the stock and cook for 10 minutes. Stir in the sliced scallions, red bell pepper, and bamboo shoots. Cook for a further 5 minutes.

6 Pour the soup into warm bowls and serve immediately.

COOK'S TIP

Sesame oil is very strongly flavored and is, therefore, only used in small quantities.

VARIATION

For extra heat, add 1 chopped red chili or 1 tsp chili powder to the soup in step 5.

Chunky Potato & Beef Soup

This is a real winter warmer—pieces of tender beef and chunky mixed vegetables are cooked in a stock flavored with sherry.

Serves 4

INGREDIENTS

2 tbsp vegetable oil
8 ounces braising or frying steak, cut into strips
8 ounces new potatoes, halved
1 carrot, diced

2 celery stalks, sliced
2 leeks, sliced
3³/4 cups beef stock
8 baby corn cobs, sliced

1 bouquet garni
2 tbsp dry sherry
salt and pepper
chopped fresh parsley, to garnish

1 Heat the vegetable oil in a large saucepan. Add the strips of meat and cook for 3 minutes, turning constantly.

2 Add the halved potatoes, diced carrot, and sliced celery and leeks. Cook for a further 5 minutes, stirring.

3 Pour the beef stock into the saucepan and bring to a boil. Reduce the heat until the liquid is simmering, then add the sliced baby corn cobs and the bouquet garni.

4 Cook the soup for a further 20 minutes, or until the meat strips and all the vegetables are cooked through.

5 Remove the bouquet garni from the saucepan and discard. Stir the dry sherry into the soup and then season to taste with salt and pepper.

6 Pour the soup into warm bowls and garnish with the chopped fresh parsley. Serve at once, accompanied by chunks of fresh, crusty bread.

COOK'S TIP

Make double the quantity of soup and freeze the remainder in a rigid container for later use. When ready to use, leave in the refrigerator to defrost thoroughly, then heat until piping hot.

Potato & Mixed Fish Soup

Any mixture of fish is suitable for this recipe, from simple smoked and white fish to salmon or mussels, depending on the occasion.

Serves 4

INGREDIENTS

2 tbsp vegetable oil
1 pound small new potatoes, halved
1 bunch scallions, sliced
1 yellow bell pepper, sliced
2 garlic cloves, crushed
1 cup dry white wine

$2^1/_2$ cups fish stock
8 ounces white fish fillet, skinned and cubed
8 ounces smoked cod fillet, skinned and cubed

2 tomatoes, peeled, seeded, and chopped
$3^1/_2$ ounces peeled cooked shrimp
$^2/_3$ cup heavy cream
2 tbsp shredded fresh basil

1 Heat the vegetable oil in a large saucepan and add the halved potatoes, sliced scallions, bell pepper, and the garlic. Sauté gently for 3 minutes, stirring constantly.

2 Add the white wine and fish stock and bring to a boil. Reduce the heat and simmer for 10-15 minutes.

3 Add the cubed fish fillets and the tomatoes to the soup and continue to cook for 10 minutes, or until the fish is cooked through.

4 Stir in the shrimp, cream, and shredded basil and cook for 2–3 minutes. Pour the soup into warm bowls and serve.

COOK'S TIP

The basil is added at the end of the cooking time as the flavor is destroyed by heat.

VARIATION

For a soup which is slightly less rich, omit the wine and stir unsweetened yogurt into the soup instead of the heavy cream.

Potato, Mixed Bean, & Apple Salad

*Use any mixture of beans you have to hand in this recipe,
but the wider the variety, the more colorful the salad.*

Serves 4

INGREDIENTS

8 ounces new potatoes, scrubbed
  and quartered
1²/₃ cups mixed canned beans, such
  as red kidney beans, flageolet, and
  borlotti beans, drained and rinsed

1 red eating apple, diced and tossed
  in 1 tbsp lemon juice
1 small yellow bell pepper, diced
1 shallot, sliced
¹/₂ bulb fennel, sliced
oak leaf lettuce leaves

DRESSING:
1 tbsp red wine vinegar
2 tbsp olive oil
¹/₂ tbsp American mustard
1 garlic clove, crushed
2 tsp chopped fresh thyme

1 Cook the quartered potatoes in a saucepan of boiling water for 15 minutes, until tender. Drain and transfer to a mixing bowl.

2 Add the mixed beans to the potatoes with the diced apple and yellow bell pepper, and the sliced shallots and fennel. Mix well, taking care not to break up the cooked potatoes.

3 In a bowl, beat all the dressing ingredients together, then pour it on the potato salad.

4 Line a plate or salad bowl with the oak leaf lettuce and spoon the potato mixture into the center. Serve immediately.

COOK'S TIP

Canned beans are used here for convenience, but dried beans may be used instead. Soak for 8 hours or overnight, drain, and place in a saucepan. Cover with water, bring to a boil, and boil for 10 minutes, then simmer until tender.

VARIATION

Use Dijon or wholegrain mustard in place of American mustard for a different flavor.

Potato, Beet, & Cucumber Salad with Dill Dressing

The beet adds a rich color to this dish, tinting the potato an appealing pink.
Mixed with thin slices of cucumber it is a really vibrant salad.

Serves 4

INGREDIENTS

1 pound waxy potatoes, diced
4 small cooked beets, sliced
$^1/_2$ small cucumber, sliced thinly
2 large dill pickles, sliced
1 red onion, halved and sliced

dill sprigs, to garnish

DRESSING:
1 garlic clove, crushed
2 tbsp olive oil

2 tbsp red wine vinegar
2 tbsp chopped fresh dill
salt and pepper

1 Cook the diced potatoes in a saucepan of boiling water for 15 minutes, or until tender. Drain and let cool.

2 When cool, mix the potato and beet together in a bowl and set aside.

3 Line a salad platter with the slices of cucumber, dill pickles, and red onion. Spoon the potato and beet mixture into the center of the platter.

4 In a small bowl, beat all the dressing ingredients together, then pour it on the salad.

5 Serve the salad immediately, garnished with dill sprigs.

COOK'S TIP

If making the salad in advance, do not mix the beet and potatoes until just before serving, as the beet will bleed its color.

VARIATION

Line the salad platter with 2 heads of endive, separated into leaves, and arrange the cucumber, dill pickle, and red onion slices on top of the leaves.

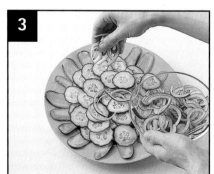

Potato, Radish, & Cucumber Salad

*The radishes and the herb and mustard dressing give this colorful salad a
mild mustard flavor which complements the potatoes perfectly.*

Serves 4

INGREDIENTS

1 pound new potatoes, scrubbed and
   halved

$^1/_2$ cucumber, sliced thinly

2 tsp salt

1 bunch radishes, sliced thinly

DRESSING:

1 tbsp Dijon mustard

2 tbsp olive oil

1 tbsp white wine vinegar

2 tbsp mixed chopped herbs

1 Cook the potatoes in a
saucepan of boiling water for
10–15 minutes, or until tender.
Drain and let cool.

2 Meanwhile spread out the
cucumber slices on a plate
and sprinkle with the salt. Let
stand for 30 minutes, then rinse
under cold running water, and pat
dry with paper towels.

3 Arrange the cucumber and
radish slices on a serving plate
in a decorative pattern and pile the
cooked potatoes in the center of
the slices.

4 In a small bowl, mix the
dressing ingredients together.
Pour the dressing on the salad,
tossing well to coat all the salad
ingredients. Chill in the
refrigerator before serving.

COOK'S TIP

*The cucumber adds not only color,
but a real freshness to the salad. It is
salted and let stand to remove the
excess water which would make the
salad soggy. Wash the cucumber
well to remove all the salt, before
adding to the salad.*

VARIATION

*Dijon mustard has a mild clean
taste, which is perfect for this salad
as it does not overpower the other
flavors. If unavailable, use another
mild mustard—English mustard is
too strong for this salad.*

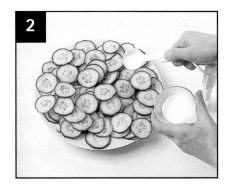

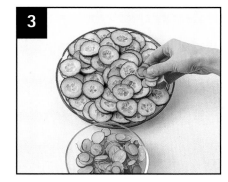

Sweet Potato & Banana Salad

This hot fruity salad combines the sweetness of the potato and the fried banana with colorful mixed bell peppers. Tossed in a honey-based dressing, it is delicious topped with crunchy croûtons.

Serves 4

INGREDIENTS

1 pound sweet potatoes, diced
10 tsp butter
1 tbsp lemon juice
1 garlic clove, crushed
1 red bell pepper, diced

1 green bell pepper, diced
2 bananas, thickly sliced
2 thick slices white bread, crusts
   removed, diced
salt and pepper

DRESSING:
2 tbsp clear honey
2 tbsp chopped fresh chives
2 tbsp lemon juice
2 tbsp olive oil

1 Cook the sweet potatoes in a saucepan of boiling water for 10–15 minutes, until tender. Drain thoroughly and reserve.

2 Meanwhile, melt the butter in a skillet. Add the lemon juice, garlic, and bell peppers and cook for 3 minutes, turning constantly.

3 Add the banana slices to the skillet and cook for 1 minute. Remove the bananas from the pan with a slotted spoon and stir into the potatoes.

4 Add the bread cubes to the skillet and cook for 2 minutes, turning frequently until they are golden brown on all sides.

5 Mix the dressing ingredients together in a small saucepan and heat the mixture until the honey is runny.

6 Spoon the potato mixture into a serving dish and season to taste with salt and pepper. Pour the dressing on the potatoes and sprinkle the croûtons over the top. Serve immediately.

COOK'S TIP

Use firm, slightly underripe bananas in this recipe as they won't turn soft and mushy when fried.

Sweet Potato & Nut Salad

Pecans with their slightly bitter flavor are mixed with sweet potatoes in this recipe to make a sweet-and-sour salad with an interesting texture.

Serves 4

INGREDIENTS

1 pound sweet potatoes, diced
2 celery stalks, sliced
1 cup grated celery root
2 scallions, sliced
1/2 cup chopped pecans
2 heads endive, separated

1 tsp lemon juice
thyme sprigs, to garnish

DRESSING:
4 tbsp vegetable oil
1 tbsp garlic wine vinegar

1 tsp light brown sugar
2 tsp chopped fresh thyme

1 Cook the sweet potatoes in a saucepan of boiling water for 5 minutes, until tender. Drain thoroughly and let cool.

2 When cooled, stir in the celery, celery root, scallions and pecans.

3 Line a salad plate with the endive leaves and sprinkle them with lemon juice.

4 Spoon the potato mixture into the center of the leaves.

5 In a small bowl, beat the dressing ingredients together.

6 Pour the dressing over the salad and serve at once, garnished with thyme sprigs.

COOK'S TIP

Sweet potatoes do not store as well as ordinary potatoes. It is best to store them in a cool, dark place (not the refrigerator) and use within 1 week of purchase.

VARIATION

For variety, replace the garlic wine vinegar in the dressing with a different flavored vinegar, such as chili or herb.

Indian Potato Salad

There are many hot Indian-flavored potato dishes which are served with curry or as part of a vegetarian meal, but this fruity salad is delicious chilled and served with nan bread or poppadoms.

Serves 4

INGREDIENTS

4 medium mealy potatoes, diced
$2^3/_4$ ounces small broccoli flowerets
1 small mango, diced
4 scallions, sliced
salt and pepper

small cooked spiced poppadoms, to
serve

DRESSING:
$^1/_2$ tsp ground cumin
$^1/_2$ tsp ground coriander

1 tbsp mango chutney
$^2/_3$ cup unsweetened yogurt
1 tsp fresh ginger root, chopped
2 tbsp chopped fresh cilantro

1 Cook the potatoes in a saucepan of boiling water for 10 minutes, or until tender. Drain and place in a mixing bowl.

2 Meanwhile, blanch the broccoli flowerets in a separate saucepan of boiling water for 2 minutes. Drain thoroughly and add to the potatoes in the bowl.

3 When the potatoes and broccoli have cooled, add the diced mango and sliced scallions.

Season to taste with salt and pepper and mix well to combine.

4 In a small bowl, stir all the dressing ingredients together.

5 Spoon the dressing on the potato mixture and mix together carefully, taking care not to break up the potatoes and broccoli.

6 Serve the salad at once, accompanied by small cooked spiced poppadoms.

COOK'S TIP

Mix the dressing ingredients together in advance and chill in the refrigerator for a few hours for a stronger flavor to develop.

Mexican Potato Salad

The flavors of Mexico are echoed in this dish where potato slices are topped with tomatoes, chilies, and ham, and served with a guacamole dressing.

Serves 4

INGREDIENTS

4 large waxy potatoes, sliced
1 ripe avocado
1 tsp olive oil
1 tsp lemon juice
1 garlic clove, crushed

1 onion, chopped
2 large tomatoes, sliced
1 green chili, chopped
1 yellow bell pepper, sliced
2 tbsp chopped fresh cilantro

salt and pepper
lemon wedges, to garnish

1 Cook the potato slices in a saucepan of boiling water for 10–15 minutes, or until tender. Drain and let cool.

2 Meanwhile, cut the avocado in half and remove the pit. Using a spoon, scoop the avocado flesh from the 2 halves and place in a mixing bowl.

3 Mash the avocado flesh with a fork and stir in the olive oil, lemon juice, garlic, and chopped onion. Cover the bowl with plastic wrap and set aside.

4 Mix the tomatoes, chili, and yellow bell pepper together and transfer to a salad bowl with the potato slices.

5 Spoon the avocado mixture on top and sprinkle with the cilantro. Season to taste and serve garnished with lemon wedges.

COOK'S TIP

Mixing the avocado flesh with lemon juice prevents it from turning brown once exposed to the air.

VARIATION

Omit the green chili from this salad if you do not like hot dishes.

Potato Nests of Chinese Salad

*Crisp fried potato nests are perfect as an edible salad bowl and delicious when
filled with a colorful Chinese-style salad of vegetables and fruit.*

Serves 4

INGREDIENTS

POTATO NESTS:
1 pound mealy potatoes, grated
1 cup cornstarch
vegetable oil, for frying
fresh chives, to garnish

SALAD:
4^1/$_2$ ounces pineapple, cubed
1 green bell pepper, cut into strips
1 carrot, cut into thin strips
1^3/$_4$ ounces snowpeas, thickly sliced
4 baby corn cobs, halved lengthwise
1 ounce bean sprouts
2 scallions, sliced

DRESSING:
1 tbsp clear honey
1 tsp light soy sauce
1 garlic clove, crushed
1 tsp lemon juice

1 To make the nests, rinse the potatoes several times in cold water. Drain well on paper towels and place them in a mixing bowl. Add the cornstarch, mixing well to coat the potatoes.

2 Half fill a wok with vegetable oil and heat until smoking. Line a 6-inch diameter wire strainer with a quarter of the potato mixture and press another strainer of the same size on top.

3 Lower the strainers into the oil and cook for 2 minutes, until the potato nest is golden and crisp. Remove from the wok, allowing the excess oil to drain off.

4 Repeat 3 more times to use up all the mixture and make a total of 4 nests. Let cool.

5 Mix the salad ingredients together in a bowl, then spoon into the potato nests.

6 Mix the dressing ingredients together in a bowl. Pour the dressing over the salad, garnish with chives, and serve.

COOK'S TIP

For this recipe, the potatoes must be washed well before use to remove excess starch. Make sure the potatoes are completely dry before cooking in the oil to prevent spitting.

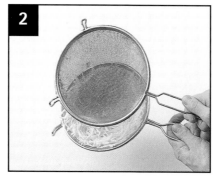

Potato, Arugula, & Apple Salad

This green and white salad is made with creamy, salty-flavored goat cheese—its distinctive flavor is perfect with salad greens.

Serves 4

INGREDIENTS

2 large potatoes, unpeeled and
   sliced
2 green eating apples, diced
1 tsp lemon juice
$^1/_4$ cup walnut pieces
$^1/_2$ cup cubed goat cheese

$5^1/_2$ ounces arugula leaves
salt and pepper

DRESSING:
2 tbsp olive oil
1 tbsp red wine vinegar

1 tsp clear honey
1 tsp fennel seeds

1 Cook the potatoes in a pan of boiling water for 15 minutes, until tender. Drain and let cool. Transfer the cooled potatoes to a serving bowl.

2 Toss the diced apples in the lemon juice, drain, and stir into the cold potatoes.

3 Add the walnut pieces, cheese cubes, and arugula leaves, then toss the salad to mix.

4 In a small bowl, beat the dressing ingredients together and pour the dressing on the salad. Serve immediately.

COOK'S TIP

Serve this salad immediately to prevent the apple from discoloring. Alternatively, prepare all the other ingredients in advance and add the apple at the last minute.

VARIATION

Use smoked or blue cheese instead of goat cheese, if you prefer. In addition, if arugula is unavailable use baby spinach instead.

Potato & Mixed Vegetable Salad with Lemon Mayonnaise

This salad is a medley of crunchy vegetables, mixed with sliced cooked potatoes and ham, then coated in a fresh-tasting lemon mayonnaise. Vary the vegetables according to availability or preference.

Serves 4

INGREDIENTS

1 pound waxy new potatoes, scrubbed
1 carrot, cut into matchsticks
8 ounces cauliflower flowerets
8 ounces baby corn cobs, halved lengthwise
6 ounces green beans

1 cup diced ham,
$^2/_3$ cup sliced mushrooms
salt and pepper

DRESSING:
2 tbsp chopped fresh parsley
$^2/_3$ cup mayonnaise

$^2/_3$ cup unsweetened yogurt
4 tsp lemon juice
rind of 1 lemon
2 tsp fennel seeds

1 Cook the potatoes in a pan of boiling water for 15 minutes, or until tender. Drain and let cool. When the potatoes are cold, slice them thinly.

2 Meanwhile, cook the carrot matchsticks, cauliflower flowerets, baby corn cobs, and green beans in a pan of boiling water for 5 minutes. Drain well and let cool.

3 Reserve 1 tsp of the chopped parsley for the garnish. In a bowl, mix the remaining dressing ingredients together.

4 Arrange the vegetables on a salad platter and top with the ham strips and sliced mushrooms.

5 Spoon the dressing over the the salad and garnish with the reserved parsley. Serve at once.

COOK'S TIP

For a really quick salad, use a frozen packet of mixed vegetables, thawed, instead of fresh vegetables.

Indonesian Potato & Chicken Salad

The spicy peanut dressing served with this salad may be prepared in advance and left to chill a day before required.

Serves 4

INGREDIENTS

4 large waxy potatoes, diced
10^1/$_2$ ounces fresh pineapple, diced
2 carrots, grated
6 ounces bean sprouts
1 bunch scallions, sliced

1 large zucchini, cut into matchsticks
3 celery stalks, cut into matchsticks
1 cup unsalted peanuts
2 cooked chicken breast fillets, about
 4^1/$_2$ ounces each, sliced

DRESSING:
6 tbsp crunchy peanut butter
6 tbsp olive oil
2 tbsp light soy sauce
1 red chili, chopped
2 tsp sesame oil
4 tsp lime juice

1 Cook the diced potatoes in a saucepan of boiling water for 10 minutes, or until tender. Drain and let cool.

2 Transfer the cooled potatoes to a salad bowl.

3 Add the pineapple, carrots, bean sprouts, scallions, zucchini, celery, peanuts, and sliced chicken to the potatoes. Toss well to mix all the salad ingredients together.

4 To make the dressing, put the peanut butter in a small bowl and gradually beat in the olive oil and light soy sauce.

5 Stir in the chopped red chili, sesame oil, and lime juice. Mix until well combined.

6 Pour the spicy dressing on the salad and toss lightly to coat all the ingredients. Serve the salad immediately, garnished with the lime wedges.

COOK'S TIP

Unsweetened canned pineapple may be used in place of the fresh pineapple for convenience. If only sweetened canned pineapple is available, drain it and rinse under cold running water before using.

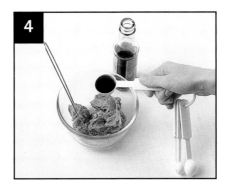

Potato & Spicy Chicken Salad

Tender chicken breast meat is perfect for salads as there is no wastage. The meat cooks quickly in small pieces and these are perfect for tossing with other salad ingredients.

Serves 4

INGREDIENTS

2 skinless chicken breast fillets, about
   $4^1/_2$ ounces each
2 tbsp butter
1 red chili, chopped
1 tbsp clear honey
$^1/_2$ tsp ground cumin

2 tbsp chopped fresh cilantro
2 large potatoes, diced
$^1/_3$ cup thin green beans, halved
1 red bell pepper, cut into thin strips
2 tomatoes, seeded and diced

DRESSING:
2 tbsp olive oil
pinch of chili powder
1 tbsp garlic wine vinegar
pinch of superfine sugar
1 tbsp chopped fresh cilantro

1 Cut the chicken into thin strips. Melt the butter in a pan over a medium heat and add the chicken, chili, honey and cumin. Cook for 10 minutes, turning until cooked through.

2 Transfer the mixture to a bowl, let cool, then stir in the cilantro.

3 Meanwhile, cook the diced potatoes in a saucepan of boiling water for 10 minutes, until tender. Drain and let cool.

4 Blanch the green beans in boiling water for 3 minutes, drain, and let cool. Mix the green beans and potatoes together in a salad bowl.

5 Add the bell pepper strips and diced tomatoes to the potatoes and beans. Stir in the spicy chicken mixture.

6 In a small bowl, beat the dressing ingredients together and pour the dressing on the salad, tossing well. Serve at once.

VARIATION

If you prefer, use lean turkey meat instead of the chicken for a slightly stronger flavor. Use the white meat for the best appearance and flavor.

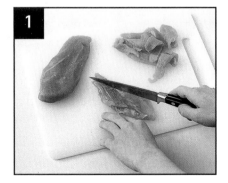

Broiled New Potato Salad

Broiled new potatoes are tossed in oil, to give them a charbroiled flavor and color. Flavored with herbs, they are served warm with a garlic mayonnaise for a delicious salad.

Serves 4

INGREDIENTS

1¹/₂ pounds new potatoes, scrubbed	salt and pepper	1 tbsp garlic wine vinegar
3 tbsp olive oil	parsley sprig, to garnish	2 garlic cloves, crushed
2 tbsp chopped fresh thyme		1 tbsp chopped fresh parsley
1 tsp paprika	DRESSING:	
4 slices smoked bacon	4 tbsp mayonnaise	

1 Cook the new potatoes in a saucepan of boiling water for 10 minutes. Drain thoroughly.

2 Mix the olive oil, chopped thyme, and paprika together and pour the mixture over the warm potatoes.

3 Place the bacon under a preheated broiler and cook for 5 minutes, turning once, until crisp. When thoroughly cooked, roughly chop the bacon and keep warm.

4 Transfer the potatoes to the broiler pan and cook for 10 minutes, turning once.

5 Mix the dressing ingredients in a small serving bowl. Transfer the potatoes and bacon to a large serving bowl. Season with salt and pepper and mix together.

6 Spoon over the dressing, garnish with a parsley sprig, and serve immediately for a warm salad. Alternatively, let cool and serve chilled.

VARIATION

Add spicy sausage to the salad in place of bacon—you do not need to cook it under the broiler before adding to the salad.

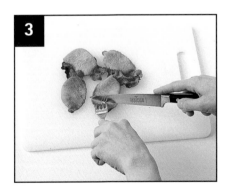

Potato & Italian Sausage Salad

Sliced Italian sausage blends well with the other Mediterranean flavors of sun-dried tomato and basil in this salad. All the flavors are relatively strong and therefore do not overpower each other.

Serves 4

INGREDIENTS

1 pound waxy potatoes
1 radicchio or lollo rosso lettuce
1 green bell pepper, sliced
6 ounces Italian sausage, sliced

1 red onion, halved and sliced
4$\frac{1}{2}$ cups sun-dried tomatoes, sliced
2 tbsp shredded fresh basil

DRESSING:
1 tbsp balsamic vinegar
1 tsp tomato paste
2 tbsp olive oil
salt and pepper

1 Cook the potatoes in a saucepan of boiling water for 20 minutes, or until cooked through. Drain and let cool.

2 Line a large serving platter with the radicchio or lollo rosso lettuce leaves.

3 Slice the cooled potatoes and arrange them in layers on the lettuce-lined serving platter, together with the sliced green bell pepper, sliced Italian sausage, red onion, sun-dried tomatoes, and shredded fresh basil.

4 In a small bowl, beat the balsamic vinegar, tomato paste, and olive oil together and season to taste with salt and pepper. Pour the dressing on the potato salad and serve immediately.

COOK'S TIP

You can use either packets of sun-dried tomatoes or jars of sun-dried tomatoes in oil. If using tomatoes packed in oil, simply rinse the oil from the tomatoes and pat them dry on paper towels before using.

VARIATION

Any sliced Italian sausage or salami can be used in this salad. Italy is the home of the salami and there are numerous varieties to choose from—those from the south tend to be more highly spiced than those from the north of the country.

Potato & Lobster Salad with Lime Dressing

The lobster makes this a special occasion salad, both in cost and flavor.
The richness of the lobster meat is offset by the tangy lime dressing.

Serves 4

INGREDIENTS

1 pound waxy potatoes, scrubbed
  and sliced
8 ounces cooked lobster meat
2/3 cup mayonnaise
2 tbsp lime juice

finely grated rind of 1 lime
1 tbsp chopped fresh parsley
2 tbsp olive oil
2 tomatoes, seeded and diced

2 hard-cooked eggs, quartered
1 tbsp quartered pitted green olives
salt and pepper

---

1 Cook the potatoes in a saucepan of boiling water for 10–15 minutes, or until cooked through. Drain and reserve.

2 Remove the lobster meat from the shell and separate it into large pieces.

3 In a bowl, mix together the mayonnaise, 1 tbsp of the lime juice, half the grated lime rind, and half the chopped parsley, then set aside.

4 In a separate bowl, beat the remaining lime juice with the olive oil and pour the dressing on the potatoes. Arrange the potatoes on a serving plate.

5 Top with the lobster meat, tomatoes, eggs, and olives. Season with salt and pepper and sprinkle with the reserved parsley.

6 Spoon the mayonnaise onto the center of the salad, top with the reserved rind, and serve.

COOK'S TIP

As shellfish is used in this salad, serve it immediately, or keep covered and chilled for up to 1 hour before serving.

VARIATION

Crab meat or shrimp may be used instead of the lobster, if you prefer.

Potato & Tuna Salad

This colorful dish is a variation of the classic Salade Niçoise. Packed with tuna and vegetables, it is both filling and delicious.

Serves 4

INGREDIENTS

1 pound new potatoes, scrubbed and quartered
1 green bell pepper, sliced
$^1/_3$ cup canned corn, drained
1 red onion, sliced

$10^1/_2$ ounces canned tuna in brine, drained and flaked
2 tbsp chopped pitted black olives
salt and pepper
lime wedges, to garnish

DRESSING:
2 tbsp mayonnaise
2 tbsp sour cream
1 tbsp lime juice
2 garlic cloves, crushed
finely grated rind of 1 lime

1 Cook the potatoes in a saucepan of boiling water for 15 minutes, until tender. Drain and let cool in a mixing bowl.

2 Gently stir in the sliced green bell pepper, corn and sliced red onion.

3 Spoon the potato mixture into a large serving bowl and arrange the flaked tuna and chopped black olives over the top. Season the salad generously with salt and pepper.

4 To make the dressing, mix together the mayonnaise, sour cream, lime juice, garlic, and lime rind in a bowl.

5 Spoon the dressing onto the tuna and olives, garnish with lime wedges, and serve.

COOK'S TIP

Served with a crisp white wine, this salad makes the perfect light lunch for summer or winter.

VARIATION

Green beans and hard-cooked egg slices can be added to the salad for a more traditional Salade Niçoise.

Snacks & Light Meals

Potatoes are so versatile that they can be used as a base to create a whole array of tempting light meals and satisfying snacks. They are also extremely nutritious, as the carbohydrate they contain will give a welcome energy boost. As potatoes have a fairly neutral flavor, they can be teamed with a variety of other ingredients and flavors to make lots of interesting meals and snacks.

This chapter contains a range of tempting snacks, including Paprika Potato Chips, Spicy Potato-filled Nan Breads, and Spanish Tortilla, which are quick and easy to make and will satisfy those mid-morning or mid-afternoon hunger pangs! They also come in handy if an expected visitor drops by.

This chapter also contains a range of delicious yet light meals which are ideal if you feel slightly peckish rather than ravenously hungry—try Potato Omelet with Feta Cheese & Spinach or Potato Pancakes with Sour Cream & Salmon.

Potato & Bean Pâté

*This pâté is easy to prepare and may be stored in the refrigerator
for up to two days. Serve with small toasts, Melba toast, or crudités.*

Serves 4

INGREDIENTS

3¹/₂ oz mealy potatoes, diced
1²/₃ cups mixed canned beans, such
   as borlotti, flageolet, and kidney
   beans, drained

1 garlic clove, crushed
2 tsp lime juice
1 tbsp chopped fresh cilantro
2 tbsp unsweetened yogurt

salt and pepper
chopped fresh cilantro, to garnish

1 Cook the potatoes in a
saucepan of boiling water for
10 minutes, until tender. Drain
well and mash.

2 Transfer the potato to a food
processor or blender and add
the beans, garlic, lime juice, and
the fresh cilantro. Season the
mixture and process for 1 minute
to make a smooth purée.
Alternatively, mix the beans with
the potato, garlic, lime juice, and
cilantro and mash.

3 Turn the purée into a bowl
and add the yogurt. Mix well.

4 Spoon the pâté into a serving
dish and garnish with the
chopped cilantro. Serve at once or
chill in the refrigerator.

COOK'S TIP

*To make Melba toast, toast ready-
sliced white or brown bread lightly
on both sides under a preheated
broiler and remove the crusts.
Holding the bread flat, slide a sharp
knife between the toasted bread to
split it horizontally. Cut into
triangles and toast the untoasted
side until the edges curl.*

VARIATION

*If you do not have a food processor
or you would prefer to make a
chunkier pâté, simply mash the
ingredients with a fork.*

Smoked Fish & Potato Pâté

This smoked fish pâté is given a tart fruity flavor by the gooseberries, which complement the fish perfectly.

Serves 4

INGREDIENTS

1¹/₂ pounds mealy potatoes, diced
10¹/₂ ounces smoked mackerel, skinned and flaked
³/₄ cup cooked gooseberries

2 tsp lemon juice
2 tbsp crème fraîche
1 tbsp capers
1 gherkin, chopped

1 tbsp chopped dill pickle
1 tbsp chopped fresh dill
salt and pepper
lemon wedges, to garnish

1 Cook the diced potatoes in a saucepan of boiling water for 10 minutes, until tender, then drain well.

2 Place the cooked potatoes in a food processor or blender.

3 Add the skinned and flaked smoked mackerel and process for 30 seconds until fairly smooth. Alternatively, mash with a fork.

4 Add the cooked gooseberries with the lemon juice and crème fraîche. Blend for a further 10 seconds or mash well.

5 Stir in the capers, gherkin, dill pickle, and chopped fresh dill. Season well with salt and pepper.

6 Turn the fish pâté into a serving dish, garnish with lemon wedges, and serve with slices of toast or warm crusty bread in chunks or slices.

COOK'S TIP

Use stewed, canned, or bottled cooked gooseberries for convenience and to save time, or when fresh gooseberries are out of season.

VARIATION

Use other tart fruits, such as stewed apples, instead of the gooseberries if they are unavailable.

Potato Kibbeh

Kibbeh is a Middle Eastern dish, traditionally made with bulgur wheat, lamb, and spices. Serve with sesame seed paste, salad, and warm Middle Eastern bread for a deliciously different snack.

Serves 4

INGREDIENTS

1 cup bulgur wheat
12 ounces mealy potatoes, diced
2 small eggs
2 tbsp butter, melted
pinch of ground cumin
pinch of ground coriander
pinch of grated nutmeg

salt and pepper
oil for deep-frying

STUFFING:
6 ounces ground lamb
1 small onion, chopped
1 tbsp pine nuts

1 ounce dried apricots, chopped
pinch of grated nutmeg
pinch of ground cinnamon
1 tbsp chopped fresh cilantro
2 tbsp lamb stock

1 Put the bulgur wheat in a bowl and cover with boiling water. Soak for 30 minutes, until the water has been absorbed and the bulgur wheat has swollen.

2 Meanwhile, cook the diced potatoes in a saucepan of boiling water for 10 minutes, or until cooked through. Drain and mash until smooth.

3 Add the bulgur wheat to the mashed potato with the eggs, the melted butter, the ground cumin and coriander, and the grated nutmeg. Season well with salt and pepper.

4 To make the stuffing, dry-fry the lamb for 5 minutes, add the onion, and cook for a further 2–3 minutes. Add the remaining stuffing ingredients and cook for 5 minutes, until the stock has been absorbed. Cool slightly, then divide into 8 portions. Roll each one into a ball.

5 Divide the potato mixture into 8 portions and flatten each into a round. Place a portion of stuffing in the center of each round. Shape the coating around the stuffing to encase it completely.

6 In a large saucepan or deep fat fryer, heat the oil to 350°F–375°F or until a cube of bread browns in 30 seconds, and cook the kibbeh for 5–7 minutes, until golden brown. Drain well and serve at once.

Potato & Meatballs in Spicy Sauce

These meatballs are delicious served with warm crusty bread to mop up the sauce. For a main meal, make half as much mixture again, rolling the balls into larger rounds; serve with rice and vegetables.

Serves 4

INGREDIENTS

8 ounces mealy potatoes, diced
8 ounces ground beef or lamb
1 onion, finely chopped
1 tbsp chopped fresh cilantro
1 celery stalk, finely chopped
2 garlic cloves, crushed
2 tbsp butter
1 tbsp vegetable oil

salt and pepper
chopped fresh cilantro,
   to garnish

SAUCE:
1 tbsp vegetable oil
1 onion, finely chopped
2 tsp light brown sugar

14 ounce can chopped tomatoes
1 green chili, chopped
1 tsp paprika
$^2/_3$ cup vegetable stock
2 tsp cornstarch

1 Cook the diced potatoes in a saucepan of boiling water for 25 minutes, until cooked through. Drain well and transfer to a large mixing bowl. Mash until smooth.

2 Add the ground beef or lamb, onion, cilantro, celery, and garlic and mix well.

3 Bring the mixture together with your hands and roll it into 20 small balls.

4 To make the sauce, heat the oil in a pan and sauté the onion for 5 minutes. Add the remaining sauce ingredients and bring to a boil, stirring. Lower the heat and simmer for 20 minutes.

5 Meanwhile, heat the butter and oil for the potato and meatballs in a skillet. Add the balls in batches and cook for 10–15 minutes, until browned, turning frequently. Keep warm

while cooking the remainder. Serve the potato and meatballs in a warm shallow ovenproof dish with the sauce poured around them and garnished with cilantro.

COOK'S TIP

Make the potato and meatballs in advance and chill or freeze them for later use. Make sure you defrost them thoroughly before cooking.

Potato & Fish Balls with Tomato Sauce

These spicy potato and fish balls are deep-fried and served with a rich tomato sauce.
Easy to prepare, they may be made in advance and fried just before eating.

Serves 4

INGREDIENTS

1 pound mealy potatoes, diced
2 smoked fish fillets, such as cod,
  about 8 ounces total weight,
  skinned
3 tbsp butter
2 eggs, beaten

1 tbsp chopped fresh dill
1/2 tsp cayenne pepper
oil for deep-frying
salt and pepper
dill sprigs, to garnish

SAUCE:
1 1/4 cups sieved tomatoes
1 tbsp tomato paste
2 tbsp chopped fresh dill
2/3 cup fish stock

1 Cook the diced potatoes in a saucepan of boiling water for 10 minutes, or until cooked. Drain well, then add the butter to the potato and mash until smooth. Season well with salt and pepper.

2 Meanwhile, poach the fish in boiling water for 10 minutes, turning once. Drain and mash the fish. Stir it into the potato mixture and let cool.

3 While the potato and fish mixture is cooling, make the sauce. Put the sieved tomatoes, tomato paste, dill, and stock in a pan and bring to a boil. Reduce the heat, cover the pan, and simmer for 20 minutes, until thickened.

4 Add the eggs, dill, and cayenne pepper to the potato and fish mixture and beat until well mixed.

5 In a large saucepan or deep-fryer, heat the oil to 350°F–375°F, or until a cube of bread browns in 30 seconds. Drop in spoons of the mixture and cook for 3–4 minutes, until golden brown. Drain on paper towels.

6 Garnish the potato and fish balls with dill sprigs and serve with the tomato sauce.

VARIATION

Smoked fish is used for extra flavor, but white fish fillets or ground shrimp may be used, if desired.

Thai Potato Crab Cakes

These small crab cakes are a variation of a traditional Thai recipe. Often found in restaurants as a starter, they are ideal as a light snack, especially when served with sweet-and-sour cucumber sauce.

Serves

INGREDIENTS

1 pound mealy potatoes, diced
6 ounces white crab meat, drained
   if canned
4 scallions, chopped
1 tsp light soy sauce
¹/₂ tsp sesame oil
1 tsp chopped lemon grass
1 tsp lime juice

3 tbsp all-purpose flour
2 tbsp vegetable oil
salt and pepper

SAUCE:
4 tbsp finely chopped cucumber
2 tbsp clear honey
1 tbsp garlic wine vinegar

¹/₂ tsp light soy sauce
1 red chili, chopped

TO GARNISH:
1 red chili, sliced
cucumber slices

1 Cook the diced potatoes in a saucepan of boiling water for 10 minutes, until cooked through. Drain well and mash.

2 Mix the crab meat into the potato with the scallions, soy sauce, sesame oil, lemon grass, lime juice, and flour. Season with salt and pepper.

3 Divide the potato mixture into 8 portions of equal size and shape them into small rounds, using floured hands.

4 Heat the oil in a wok or skillet and cook the cakes, 4 at a time, for 5–7 minutes, turning once. Keep warm and repeat with the remaining mixture.

5 Meanwhile, make the sauce. In a small serving bowl, mix the cucumber, honey, vinegar, soy sauce, and chopped red chili.

6 Garnish the cakes with the sliced red chili and cucumber slices and serve with the sauce.

COOK'S TIP

Do not make the cucumber sauce too far in advance as the water from the cucumber will make the sauce runny and dilute the flavor.

Potato & Mixed Mushroom Patties

These patties will be loved by vegetarians and meat-eaters alike. Packed with creamy potato and as wide a variety of mushrooms as you wish to use, they are delicious served with a simple crisp salad.

Serves 4

INGREDIENTS

1 pound mealy potatoes, diced
2 tbsp butter
6 ounces mixed mushrooms, chopped
2 garlic cloves, crushed

1 small egg, beaten
1 tbsp chopped fresh chives, plus
 extra to garnish
flour, for dusting

oil, for frying
salt and pepper

1 Cook the potatoes in a pan of boiling water for 10 minutes, or until cooked through. Drain well, mash, and set aside.

2 Meanwhile, melt the butter in a skillet and cook the mushrooms and garlic for 5 minutes, stirring. Drain well.

3 Stir the mushrooms and garlic into the potato, together with the beaten egg and chives.

4 Divide the mixture equally into 4 portions and shape them into round patties. Toss them in the flour until the outsides are completely coated.

5 Heat the oil in a skillet and cook the potato patties over a medium heat for 10 minutes, until they are golden brown, turning them over halfway through. Serve the cakes at once, with a salad.

VARIATION

If chives are unavailable, use other fresh herbs of your choice. Sage, tarragon, and cilantro all combine well with mixed mushrooms.

COOK'S TIP

Prepare the cakes in advance, cover, and chill in the refrigerator for up to 24 hours, if desired.

Potato, Cheese, & Onion Rosti

These grated potato patties are also known as straw cakes, as they resemble a straw mat! Serve them with a tomato sauce or salad for a light supper dish.

Serves 4

INGREDIENTS

2 pounds Maris Piper, or other main crop potato

1 onion, grated

1/2 cup grated Swiss cheese

2 tbsp chopped fresh parsley

1 tbsp olive oil

2 tbsp butter

salt and pepper

TO GARNISH:

shredded scallion

1 small tomato, quartered

1 Parboil the potatoes in a pan of boiling water for 10 minutes, drain, and let cool. Peel the potatoes and grate with a coarse grater. Place the grated potatoes in a large mixing bowl.

2 Stir in the onion, cheese, and parsley. Season well with salt and pepper. Divide the potato mixture into 4 portions of equal size and form them into patties.

3 Heat half of the olive oil and butter in a skillet and cook 2 of the potato patties over a high heat for 1 minute, then reduce the heat and cook for 5 minutes, until they are golden underneath. Turn them over and cook for a further 5 minutes.

4 Repeat with the other half of the oil and butter to cook the remaining 2 patties. Transfer to serving plates, garnish, and serve.

COOK'S TIP

The potato patties should be flattened as much as possible during cooking, otherwise the outside will be cooked before the center.

VARIATION

To make these rosti into a more substantial meal, add chopped cooked bacon or ham to the potato mixture.

Potato & Cauliflower Fritters

These fritters make a filling snack. They are a great way to use up leftover cooked vegetables if you have any to hand, as they are delicious made with virtually any vegetables.

Serves 4

INGREDIENTS

8 ounces mealy potatoes, diced
8 ounces cauliflower flowerets
2 tbsp grated Parmesan cheese

1 egg
1 egg white for coating
oil, for frying

paprika, for dusting (optional)
salt and pepper
crispy bacon slices, chopped, to serve

1 Cook the potatoes in a saucepan of boiling water for 10 minutes, until cooked through. Drain well and mash.

2 Cook the cauliflower flowerets in a separate pan of boiling water for 10 minutes.

3 Drain the cauliflower flowerets and mix into the mashed potato. Stir in the grated Parmesan cheese and season well with salt and pepper.

4 Separate the whole egg and beat the yolk into the potato and cauliflower, mixing well.

5 Lightly beat both the egg whites in a clean bowl, then carefully fold into the potato and cauliflower mixture.

6 Divide the potato mixture into 8 equal portions and shape them into rounds.

7 Heat the oil in a skillet and cook the fritters for 3–5 minutes, turning once halfway through cooking.

8 Dust the cooked fritters with a little paprika, if desired, and serve at once accompanied by the crispy chopped bacon.

VARIATION

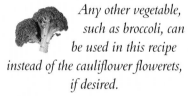

Any other vegetable, such as broccoli, can be used in this recipe instead of the cauliflower flowerets, if desired.

Potato Fritters with Garlic Sauce

*Chunks of cooked potato are coated first in Parmesan cheese, then in a
light batter before being fried until golden for a hot vegetarian snack.*

Serves 4

INGREDIENTS

1 pound waxy potatoes, cut into
  large cubes
1¹/₂ cups grated Parmesan cheese
oil, for deep-frying

SAUCE:
2 tbsp butter
1 onion, halved and sliced
2 garlic cloves, crushed
¹/₄ cup all-purpose flour
1¹/₄ cups milk
1 tbsp chopped fresh parsley

BATTER:
¹/₂ cup all-purpose flour
1 small egg
²/₃ cup milk

1 To make the sauce, melt the butter in a saucepan and cook the sliced onion and garlic for 2–3 minutes. Add the flour and cook for 1 minute.

2 Remove from the heat and stir in the milk and parsley. Return to the heat and bring to a boil. Keep warm.

3 Meanwhile, cook the cubed potatoes in a saucepan of boiling water for 5–10 minutes, until just firm. Do not overcook or they will fall apart.

4 Drain the potatoes and toss them in the Parmesan cheese.

5 To make the batter, place the flour in a mixing bowl and gradually beat in the egg and milk until smooth. Dip the potato cubes into the batter to coat them.

6 In a large saucepan or deep-fryer, heat the oil to 350°F–375°F, or until a cube of bread browns in 30 seconds, and cook the fritters for 3–4 minutes, or until golden. Drain the fritters with a slotted spoon and transfer them to a serving bowl. Serve with the sauce.

COOK'S TIP

*Coat the potatoes in the Parmesan
while still slightly wet to ensure that
the cheese sticks and coats well.*

Potato Croquettes with Ham & Cheese

This is a classic potato dish which may be served plain as an accompaniment, or with added ingredients, such as other cooked vegetables or salami, and a cheese sauce as a snack.

Serves 4

INGREDIENTS

1 pound mealy potatoes, diced
1$^{1}/_{2}$ cups milk
2 tbsp butter
4 scallions, chopped
2$^{3}/_{4}$ ounces Cheddar cheese
1$^{3}/_{4}$ ounces smoked ham, chopped
1 celery stalk, diced
1 egg, beaten

$^{1}/_{2}$ cup all-purpose flour
oil, for deep frying
salt and pepper

COATING:
2 eggs, beaten
2$^{1}/_{4}$ cups fresh whole-wheat bread
   crumbs

SAUCE:
2 tbsp butter
$^{1}/_{4}$ cup all-purpose flour
$^{2}/_{3}$ cup milk
$^{2}/_{3}$ cup vegetable stock
$^{2}/_{3}$ cup Cheddar cheese, grated
1 tsp Dijon mustard
1 tbsp chopped cilantro

1 Place the potatoes in a pan with the milk and bring to a boil. Reduce to a simmer until the liquid has been absorbed and the potatoes are cooked.

2 Add the butter and mash the potatoes. Stir in the scallions, cheese, ham, celery, egg, and flour. Season with salt and pepper to taste and let cool.

3 To make the coating, beat the eggs in a bowl. Put the bread crumbs in a separate bowl.

4 Shape the potato mixture into 8 balls. First dip them in the egg, then in the bread crumbs.

5 To make the sauce, melt the butter in a small pan. Add the flour and cook for 1 minute.

Remove from the heat and stir in the milk, stock, cheese, mustard, and herbs. Bring to a boil, stirring until thickened. Reduce the heat and keep warm.

6 In a deep -fryer, heat the oil to 350°F–375°F and fry the croquettes for 5 minutes, until golden. Drain well and serve with the sauce.

Hash Browns with Tomato Sauce

Hash Browns are a popular recipe of fried potato squares, often served as brunch.
This recipe includes extra vegetables for a more substantial snack.

Serves 4

INGREDIENTS

1 pound waxy potatoes
1 carrot, diced
1 celery stalk, diced
$^3/_4$ cup diced button mushrooms
1 onion, diced
2 garlic cloves, crushed
1 ounce frozen peas, thawed
$^2/_3$ cup grated Parmesan cheese

4 tbsp vegetable oil
2 tbsp butter
salt and pepper

SAUCE:
$1^1/_4$ cups sieved tomatoes
2 tbsp chopped fresh cilantro
1 tbsp Worcestershire sauce

$^1/_2$ tsp chili powder
2 tsp brown sugar
2 tsp American mustard
$^1/_3$ cup vegetable stock

1 Cook the potatoes in a saucepan of boiling water for 10 minutes. Drain and let cool. Meanwhile, cook the carrot in boiling water for 5 minutes.

2 When cool, grate the potato with a coarse grater.

3 Drain the carrot and add it to the grated potato with the celery, mushrooms, onion, peas, and cheese. Season well.

4 Place all the sauce ingredients in a pan and bring to a boil. Reduce the heat and simmer for 15 minutes.

5 Divide the potato mixture into 8 portions of equal size and shape into flattened rectangles with your hands.

6 Heat the oil and butter in a skillet and cook the hash browns over a low heat for

4–5 minutes on each side, until crisp and golden brown.

7 Serve the hash browns with the tomato sauce.

COOK'S TIP

Use any mixture of vegetables for this recipe. For a nonvegetarian dish, add bacon pieces or diced ham for added flavor.

Potato Pancakes with Sour Cream & Salmon

These pancakes are based on the latke, *which is traditionally a thin, crisp pancake. In this recipe, the pancakes are served with smoked salmon and sour cream for a little taste of luxury.*

Serves 4

INGREDIENTS

1 pound mealy potatoes, grated	2 tbsp vegetable oil	TOPPING:
2 scallions, chopped	salt and pepper	$^2/_3$ cup sour cream
2 tbsp self-rising flour	fresh chives, to garnish	$4^1/_2$ ounces smoked salmon
2 eggs, beaten		

1 Rinse the grated potatoes under cold running water, drain, and pat dry on paper towels. Transfer to a mixing bowl.

2 Mix the chopped scallions, flour, and eggs into the potatoes and season well with salt and pepper.

3 Heat 1 tbsp of the oil in a skillet. Drop about 4 tablespoonfuls of the mixture into the pan and spread each one with the back of a spoon to form a round (the mixture should make 16 pancakes). Cook for 5–7 minutes, turning once, until golden. Drain well.

4 Heat the remaining oil and cook the remaining mixture in batches.

5 Top the pancakes with the sour cream and smoked salmon, garnish with fresh chives, and serve hot.

COOK'S TIP

Smaller versions of this dish may be made and served as appetizers.

VARIATION

These pancakes are equally delicious topped with prosciutto or any other dry-cured ham instead of the smoked salmon.

Potato Omelet with Feta Cheese & Spinach

This quick, chunky omelet has pieces of potato cooked into the egg mixture and is then folded and filled with a classic combination of feta cheese and spinach.

Serves 4

INGREDIENTS

$^1/_3$ cup butter

6 waxy potatoes, diced

3 garlic cloves, crushed

1 tsp paprika

2 tomatoes, skinned, seeded, and diced

12 eggs

pepper

FILLING:

8 ounces baby spinach

1 tsp fennel seeds

1 cup diced feta cheese

4 tbsp unsweetened yogurt

1 Heat 2 tbsp of the butter in a skillet and cook the potatoes over a low heat for 7–10 minutes, until golden, stirring constantly. Transfer to a bowl.

2 Add the garlic, paprika, and tomatoes and cook for a further 2 minutes.

3 Beat the eggs together and season with pepper. Pour the eggs into the potato mixture and mix well.

4 Place the spinach in boiling water for 1 minute, until just wilted. Drain, rinse the spinach under cold running water, and pat dry with paper towels. Stir in the fennel seeds, feta cheese and yogurt.

5 Heat 1 tbsp of the butter in a 6-inch omelet pan or skillet. Ladle a quarter of the egg and potato mixture into the pan. Cook for 2 minutes, turning once, until just set.

6 Transfer the omelet to a serving plate. Spoon a quarter of the spinach mixture onto one half of the omelet, then fold the omelet in half over the filling. Repeat to make 4 omelets.

VARIATION

Use any other cheese, such as blue cheese, instead of the feta, and blanched broccoli in place of the baby spinach, if you prefer.

Spanish Tortilla

This classic Spanish dish is often served as part of a tapas (appetizer) selection. A variety of cooked vegetables can be added to this recipe, making it an ideal way to use up leftovers.

Serves 4

INGREDIENTS

2¹/₄ pounds waxy potatoes,
   thinly sliced
4 tbsp vegetable oil
1 onion, sliced
2 garlic cloves, crushed

1 green bell pepper, diced
2 tomatoes, seeded and
   chopped
1 ounce canned corn,
   drained

6 large eggs, beaten
2 tbsp chopped fresh parsley
salt and pepper

1 Parboil the potatoes in a saucepan of boiling water for 5 minutes. Drain well.

2 Heat the oil in a large skillet, add the potato and onions, and sauté gently for 5 minutes, stirring constantly, until the potatoes have browned.

3 Add the garlic, diced bell pepper, chopped tomatoes, and corn, mixing well.

4 Pour in the eggs and add the chopped parsley. Season well with salt and pepper. Cook for 10–12 minutes, until the underside is cooked through.

5 Remove the skillet from the heat and continue to cook the tortilla under a preheated broiler for 5–7 minutes, or until the tortilla is set and the top is golden brown.

6 Cut the tortilla into wedges or cubes, depending on your preference, and serve with salad. In Spain tortillas are served hot, cold, or warm.

COOK'S TIP

Ensure that the handle of your skillet is heatproof before placing it under the broiler and be sure to use potholders when removing it as it will be very hot.

Paprika Chips

These wafer-thin potato crisps are great cooked over a barbecue and served with spicy chicken or pork. They also work well broiled, but they do not take on the smoky flavor.

Serves

INGREDIENTS

2 large potatoes
3 tbsp olive oil

¹/₂ tsp paprika pepper

salt

1 Using a sharp knife, slice the potatoes very thinly so that they are almost transparent. Drain the potato slices thoroughly and pat dry with paper towels.

2 Heat the oil in a large skillet and add the paprika, stirring constantly, to ensure that the paprika doesn't catch and burn on the bottom of the pan.

3 Add the potato slices to the skillet and cook them in a single layer for about 5 minutes, or until the potato slices just begin to brown and curl slightly at the edges.

4 Remove the potato slices from the pan using a slotted spoon. Transfer them to paper towels and pat dry to drain thoroughly.

5 Thread the potato slices on to several wooden kabob skewers.

6 Sprinkle the potato slices with a little salt and cook over a medium hot barbecue or under a preheated broiler for 10 minutes, turning frequently, until the potato slices begin to crispen. Sprinkle with a little more salt, if desired, and serve.

VARIATION

You could use curry powder or any other spice to flavor the chips instead of the paprika, if desired.

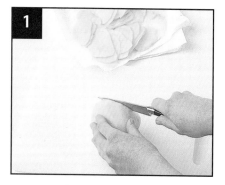
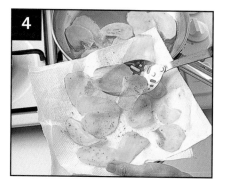

Creamy Mushrooms & Potatoes

These oven-baked mushrooms are filled with a creamy potato and mushroom mixture topped with melted cheese. Served with crisp salad greens, they make a delicious light meal.

Serves 4

INGREDIENTS

1 ounce dried porcini, or other dried wild mushrooms

8 ounces mealy potatoes, diced

2 tbsp butter, melted

4 tbsp heavy cream

2 tbsp chopped fresh chives

$^1/_4$ cup grated Swiss cheese

8 large open-capped mushrooms

$^2/_3$ cup vegetable stock

salt and pepper

fresh chives, to garnish

1 Place the dried porcini in a bowl, cover with boiling water, and soak for 20 minutes.

2 Meanwhile, cook the potatoes in a saucepan of boiling water for 10 minutes, until cooked. Drain well and mash.

3 Drain the soaked porcini and chop them finely. Mix them into the mashed potato.

4 Mix the butter, cream, and chives together and add to the porcini and potato mixture. Season with salt and pepper.

5 Remove the stalks from the open-capped mushrooms. Chop the stalks and stir them into the potato mixture. Spoon the mixture into the open-capped mushrooms and sprinkle the cheese over the top.

6 Place the filled mushrooms in a shallow ovenproof dish and pour in the vegetable stock.

7 Cover the dish and cook in a preheated oven at 425°F for 20 minutes. Remove the lid and cook for 5 minutes, until golden on top.

8 Garnish the mushrooms with fresh chives and serve at once.

VARIATION

Use fresh mushrooms instead of the dried porcini, if preferred, and stir a mixture of chopped nuts into the mushroom stuffing mixture for extra crunch.

Potato Noodles with Cheese, Mushrooms, & Bacon

In this recipe, potatoes are used to make a "pasta" dough, which is cut into thin noodles and boiled. The noodles are served with a creamy bacon and mushroom sauce.

Serves 4

INGREDIENTS

1 pound mealy potatoes, diced	SAUCE:	3 smoked bacon slices, chopped
2 cups all-purpose flour	1 tbsp vegetable oil	$^2/_3$ cup grated Parmesan cheese
1 egg, beaten	1 onion, chopped	$1^1/_4$ cups heavy cream
1 tbsp milk	1 garlic clove, crushed	2 tbsp chopped fresh parsley
salt and pepper		
parsley sprig, to garnish	2 cups sliced open-capped	
	mushrooms	

1 Cook the diced potatoes in a saucepan of boiling water for 10 minutes, until cooked through. Drain well. Mash the potatoes until smooth, then beat in the flour, egg, and milk. Season with salt and pepper and bring together to form a stiff paste.

2 On a lightly floured surface, roll out the paste to form a thin sausage shape. Cut the sausage into 1-inch lengths. Bring a large pan of salted water to a boil, drop in the dough pieces, and cook for 3–4 minutes. They will rise to the top when cooked.

3 To make the sauce, heat the oil in a pan and sauté the onion and garlic for 2 minutes. Add the mushrooms and bacon and cook for 5 minutes. Stir in the cheese, cream, and parsley and season.

4 Drain the noodles and transfer to a warm pasta bowl. Spoon the sauce over the top and toss to mix. Garnish with a parsley sprig and serve.

COOK'S TIP

Make the dough in advance, then wrap, and store the noodles in the refrigerator for up to 24 hours.

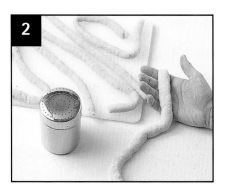

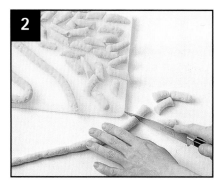

Potato & Mushroom Bake

Use any mixture of mushrooms to hand for this creamy layered bake.
It can be served straight from the dish in which it is cooked.

Serves 4

INGREDIENTS

2 tbsp butter
1 pound waxy potatoes, thinly sliced
2 cups sliced mixed mushrooms

1 tbsp chopped fresh rosemary
4 tbsp chopped fresh chives
2 garlic cloves, crushed

^{2}/$_3$ cup heavy cream
salt and pepper
fresh chives, to garnish

1 Grease a shallow, round ovenproof dish with butter.

2 Parboil the sliced potatoes in a saucepan of boiling water for 10 minutes. Drain well. Layer a quarter of the potatoes in the base of the dish.

3 Arrange a quarter of the mushrooms on top of the potatoes and sprinkle with a quarter of the rosemary, chives, and garlic.

4 Continue layering in the same order, finishing with a layer of potatoes on top.

5 Pour the cream over the top of the potatoes. Season well.

6 Cook in a preheated oven at 375°F for 45 minutes, or until the bake is golden brown.

7 Garnish with fresh chives and serve at once.

COOK'S TIP

For a special occasion, the bake may be made in a lined cake pan and turned out to serve.

VARIATION

Use 2 ounces re-hydrated dried mushrooms instead of the fresh mixed mushrooms, for a really intense flavor.

Spicy Potato-Filled Nan Breads

This is a filling Indian sandwich. Spicy potatoes fill the nan breads,
which are served with a cool cucumber raita and lime pickle.

Serves 4

INGREDIENTS

8 ounces waxy potatoes, scrubbed
   and diced
1 tbsp vegetable oil
1 onion, chopped
2 garlic cloves, crushed
1 tsp ground cumin
1 tsp ground coriander

$^1/_2$ tsp chili powder
1 tbsp tomato paste
3 tbsp vegetable stock
$2^3/_4$ ounces baby spinach, shredded
4 small or 2 large nan breads
lime pickle, to serve

RAITA:
$^2/_3$ cup unsweetened yogurt
4 tbsp diced cucumber
1 tbsp chopped mint

1 Cook the diced potatoes in a saucepan of boiling water for 10 minutes. Drain thoroughly.

2 Heat the vegetable oil in a separate saucepan and cook the onion and garlic for 3 minutes, stirring. Add the spices and cook for a further 2 minutes.

3 Stir in the potatoes, tomato paste, vegetable stock, and spinach. Cook for 5 minutes, until the potatoes are tender.

4 Warm the nan breads in a preheated oven at 300°F for about 2 minutes.

5 To make the raita, mix the yogurt, cucumber, and mint together in a small bowl.

6 Remove the nan breads from the oven. Using a sharp knife, cut a pocket in the side of each naan bread. Spoon the spicy potato filling mixture into each naan bread pocket.

7 Serve the filled nan breads at once, accompanied by the raita and lime pickle.

COOK'S TIP

To give the raita a much stronger flavor, make it in advance and chill in the refrigerator until ready to serve.

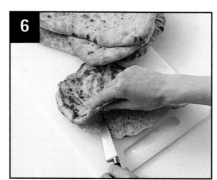

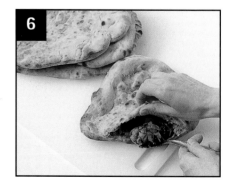

Potato & Spinach Filo Triangles

These small pasties are made with crisp filo pastry and filled with a delicious spinach and potato mixture flavored with chili and tomato. Serve hot or cold with the lemon mayonnaise.

Serves 4

INGREDIENTS

8 ounces waxy potatoes, diced finely
1 pound baby spinach
1 tomato, seeded and chopped
1/4 tsp chili powder

1/2 tsp lemon juice
8 ounces packet filo pastry, thawed if frozen
2 tbsp butter, melted
salt and pepper

MAYONNAISE:
2/3 cup mayonnaise
2 tsp lemon juice
rind of 1 lemon

1 Lightly grease a cookie sheet with a little butter.

2 Cook the potatoes in a saucepan of boiling water for 10 minutes, or until cooked through. Drain thoroughly and place in a mixing bowl.

3 Meanwhile, put the spinach in a saucepan with 2 tbsp of water, cover, and cook over a low heat for 2 minutes, until wilted. Drain the spinach thoroughly and add to the potato.

4 Stir in the chopped tomato, chili powder, and lemon juice. Season to taste with salt and pepper.

5 Lightly butter 8 sheets of filo pastry. Spread out 4 of the sheets and lay the other 4 on top of each. Cut them into 8 x 4-inch rectangles.

6 Spoon the potato and spinach mixture onto one end of each rectangle. Fold a corner of the pastry over the filling, fold the pointed end back over the pastry

strip, then fold over the remaining pastry to form a triangle.

7 Place the triangles on the cookie sheet and bake in a preheated oven at 375°F for 20 minutes, or until a golden brown color.

8 To make the mayonnaise, mix the mayonnaise, lemon juice, and lemon rind together in a small bowl. Serve the potato and spinach filo triangles warm or cold with the lemon mayonnaise and crisp salad greens.

Side Dishes

When the potato is thought of as a component of a meal, it is inevitably associated with meat and vegetables, and is served either roasted or boiled. In fact, the potato is so versatile in its ability to combine with other flavorings and be cooked in so many different ways that it is the perfect base for a whole variety of delicious side dishes. This chapter demonstrates that versatility with a wide range of tantalizing recipes.

Potatoes can be cooked and served in many different ways, such as mashing, roasting, stir-frying, pan-frying, deep-frying, baking, and boiling. You will find all kinds of different recipes for side dishes in this chapter, including Candied Sweet Potatoes, Spanish Potatoes, Thai Potato Stir-fry, and Steamed Potatoes En Papillotes. There are also classic recipes, such as Potatoes Dauhinoise and Pommes Anna, as well as updated versions of traditional dishes, such as Chili Roast Potatoes and Spicy Potato Fries. The variety is endless!

Colcannon

This is an old Irish recipe, usually served with a piece of bacon,
but it is equally delicious with chicken or fish.

Serves 4

INGREDIENTS

2¹/₂ cups shredded green cabbage
¹/₃ cup milk
8 oz mealy potatoes, diced

1 large leek, chopped
pinch of grated nutmeg

1 tbsp butter, melted
salt and pepper

1 Cook the shredded cabbage in a saucepan of boiling salted water for 7–10 minutes. Drain thoroughly and set aside.

2 Meanwhile, in a separate saucepan, bring the milk to a boil and add the potatoes and leek. Reduce the heat and simmer for 15–20 minutes, or until they are cooked through.

3 Stir in the grated nutmeg and mash the potatoes and leeks together.

4 Add the drained cabbage to the potatoes and mix well.

5 Spoon the potato and cabbage mixture into a serving dish, making a hollow in the center with the back of a spoon.

6 Pour the melted butter into the hollow and serve the dish immediately.

COOK'S TIP

There are many different varieties
of cabbage, which produce hearts
at varying times of year, so you
can be sure of being able to make
this delicious cabbage dish all
year round.

VARIATION

Add diced cooked bacon to the
recipe for extra flavor, adding it
with the leeks and cabbage.

Candied Sweet Potatoes

A taste of the Caribbean is introduced in this recipe, where sweet potatoes are cooked with sugar and lime with a dash of brandy.

Serves 4

INGREDIENTS

1^1/$_2$ pounds sweet potatoes, sliced
3 tbsp butter

1 tbsp lime juice
^{1}/$_2$ cup dark brown sugar

1 tbsp brandy
grated rind of 1 lime
lime wedges, to garnish

1 Cook the sweet potatoes in a saucepan of boiling water for 5 minutes. Test the potatoes have softened by pricking with a fork. Remove the sweet potatoes with a slotted spoon and drain thoroughly.

2 Melt the butter in a large skillet. Add the lime juice and brown sugar and heat gently to dissolve the sugar.

3 Stir the sweet potatoes and the brandy into the sugar and lime juice mixture. Cook over a low heat for 10 minutes, until the potato slices are cooked through.

4 Sprinkle the lime rind over the top of the sweet potatoes and mix well.

5 Transfer the candied sweet potatoes to a serving plate. Garnish with lime wedges and serve at once.

VARIATION

This dish may be prepared with waxy potatoes instead of sweet potatoes, if you prefer. Cook the potatoes for 10 minutes in step 1, instead of 5 minutes. Follow the same cooking method.

VARIATION

Serve this dish with spicy meats to complement the sweetness of the potatoes, if desired.

COOK'S TIP

Sweet potatoes have a pinkish skin and either white, yellow, or orange flesh. It doesn't matter which type is used for this dish.

Potatoes with Onion & Herbs

Fried potatoes are a classic favorite; here they are given extra flavor by precooking the potatoes and shallow frying them in butter with onion, garlic, and herbs.

Serves 4

INGREDIENTS

2 pounds waxy potatoes, cut into cubes
1/2 cup butter

1 red onion, cut into 8
2 garlic cloves, crushed
1 tsp lemon juice

2 tbsp chopped fresh thyme
salt and pepper

1 Cook the cubed potatoes in a saucepan of boiling water for 10 minutes. Drain thoroughly.

2 Melt the butter in a large, heavy-based skillet and add the red onion wedges, garlic, and lemon juice. Cook for 2–3 minutes, stirring.

3 Add the potatoes to the pan and mix well to coat in the butter mixture.

4 Reduce the heat, cover the skillet, and cook for 25–30 minutes, or until the potatoes are golden and tender.

5 Sprinkle the chopped thyme over the top of the potatoes and season with salt and pepper to taste.

6 Serve immediately as a side dish to accompany broiled meats or fish.

COOK'S TIP

Keep checking the potatoes and stirring throughout the cooking time to ensure that they do not burn or stick to the base of the skillet.

COOK'S TIP

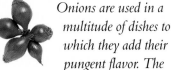

Onions are used in a multitude of dishes to which they add their pungent flavor. The beautifully colored purple-red onions used here have a mild, slightly sweet flavor, as well as looking extremely attractive. Because of their mild taste, they are equally good eaten raw in salads .

Caramelized New Potatoes

This simple recipe is best served with plainly cooked pork or chicken as it is fairly sweet and has delicious juices which complement the flavors of these meats.

Serves 4

INGREDIENTS

1¹/₂ pounds new potatoes, scrubbed
4 tbsp dark brown sugar
¹/₄ cup butter

1 tbsp orange juice
1 tbsp chopped fresh parsley or
   cilantro

salt and pepper
orange rind curls, to garnish

1 Cook the new potatoes in a saucepan of boiling water for 10 minutes, or until almost tender. Drain thoroughly.

2 Melt the sugar in a large, heavy-based skillet over a low heat, stirring.

3 Add the butter and orange juice to the pan, stirring the mixture as the butter melts.

4 Add the potatoes to the orange and butter mixture and continue to cook, turning the potatoes frequently until they are completely coated in the caramel.

5 Sprinkle the chopped parsley or cilantro over the potatoes and season to taste with salt and pepper.

6 Transfer the caramelized new potatoes to a serving dish and garnish with the orange rind. Serve immediately.

COOK'S TIP

Heat the sugar and butter gently, stirring constantly, to make sure that the mixture doesn't burn or stick to the base of the skillet.

VARIATION

Lemon or lime juices may be used instead of the orange juice, if desired. In addition, garnish the finished dish with pared lemon or lime rind, if preferred.

Spanish Potatoes

This type of dish is usually served as part of a Spanish tapas, and is delicious with salad or broiled, plain meat.

Serves 4

INGREDIENTS

2 tbsp olive oil
1 pound small new potatoes, halved
1 onion, halved and sliced
1 green bell pepper, cut into strips

1 tsp chili powder
1 tsp prepared mustard
1¹/₄ cups sieved tomatoes
1¹/₄ cups vegetable stock

salt and pepper
chopped fresh parsley, to garnish

1 Heat the olive oil in a skillet and add the halved new potatoes and the sliced onion. Cook for 4–5 minutes, stirring frequently, until the onion slices have just softened.

2 Add the green bell pepper strips, chili powder, and mustard to the pan and cook for a further 2–3 minutes.

3 Stir the sieved tomatoes and the vegetable stock into the pan and bring to a boil. Reduce the heat and cook the mixture for about 25 minutes, or until the potatoes are tender.

4 Transfer the potatoes to a serving dish. Sprinkle the parsley over the top of the potatoes and serve hot. Alternatively, let the Spanish potatoes cool completely and serve cold.

COOK'S TIP

In Spain, tapas are traditionally served with a glass of chilled sherry or some other aperitif.

COOK'S TIP

The array of little appetizer snacks known as tapas are a traditional Spanish social custom. Spaniards often visit several bars throughout the evening eating different tapas, ranging from stuffed olives and salted almonds, to slices of ham and deep-fried squid rings.

Spicy Indian Potatoes with Spinach

The potato is widely used in Indian cooking and there are many variations of spicy potatoes. In this recipe, spinach is added for both color and flavor.

Serves 4

INGREDIENTS

$^{1}/_{2}$ tsp coriander seeds
1 tsp cumin seeds
4 tbsp vegetable oil
2 cardamom pods
$^{1}/_{2}$-inch piece fresh ginger root, grated

1 red chili, chopped
1 onion, chopped
2 garlic cloves, crushed
1 pound new potatoes, quartered
$^{2}/_{3}$ cup vegetable stock
$1^{1}/_{2}$ pounds spinach, chopped

4 tbsp unsweetened yogurt
salt

1 Grind the coriander and cumin seeds using a pestle and mortar.

2 Heat the oil in a skillet. Add the ground coriander and cumin seeds to the pan, together with the cardamom pods and ginger and cook for about 2 minutes.

3 Add the chopped chili, onion, and garlic to the pan. Cook for a further 2 minutes, stirring frequently.

4 Add the potatoes to the pan, together with the vegetable stock. Cook gently for 30 minutes, or until the potatoes are cooked through, stirring occasionally.

5 Add the spinach to the pan and cook for a further 5 minutes.

6 Remove the pan from the heat and stir in the yogurt. Season with salt and pepper to taste. Transfer the potatoes and spinach to a serving dish and serve.

VARIATION

Use frozen spinach instead of fresh spinach, if you prefer. Defrost the frozen spinach and drain it thoroughly before adding it to the dish, otherwise it will turn soggy.

COOK'S TIP

This spicy dish is ideal served with a meat curry or alternatively, as part of a vegetarian meal.

Potatoes & Mushrooms in Red Wine

This is a rich recipe which is best served with plain dark meats,
such as beef or game, to complement the flavor.

Serves 4

INGREDIENTS

¹/₂ cup butter	8 shallots, halved	salt and pepper
1 pound new potatoes, halved	2 cups oyster mushrooms	sage leaves or cilantro sprigs, to
³/₄ cup red wine	1 tbsp chopped fresh sage or cilantro	garnish
¹/₃ cup beef stock		

1 Melt the butter in a heavy-based skillet and add the halved potatoes. Cook gently for 5 minutes, stirring constantly.

2 Add the red wine, beef stock, and halved shallots. Season to taste with salt and pepper and then simmer for 30 minutes.

3 Stir in the mushrooms and chopped sage or cilantro and cook for 5 minutes.

4 Turn the potatoes and mushrooms into a warm serving dish. Garnish with sage leaves or cilantro sprigs and serve at once.

COOK'S TIP

Oyster mushrooms may be grey, yellow, or red in color. They have a soft, melting texture and mild flavor. As they cook, they emit a lot of liquid and shrink to about half their original size. They require little cooking before they start to turn mushy, so add them at the end of the cooking time.

VARIATION

If oyster mushrooms are unavailable, other mushrooms, such as large open-cap mushrooms, can be used instead.

Gingered Potatoes

This is a simple spicy dish which is ideal with broiled meat or fish.
The cashews and celery add extra crunch.

Serves 4

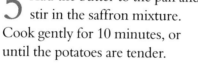

1¹/₂ pounds waxy potatoes, cubed

2 tbsp vegetable oil

2-inch piece fresh ginger root, grated

1 green chili, chopped

1 celery stalk, chopped

¹/₄ cup cashews

few strands of saffron

3 tbsp boiling water

¹/₄ cup butter

celery leaves, to garnish

1 Cook the potatoes in a saucepan of boiling water for 10 minutes. Drain thoroughly.

2 Heat the oil in a heavy-based skillet and add the potatoes. Cook for 3-4 minutes, stirring constantly.

3 Add the grated ginger, chili, celery, and cashews and cook for 1 minute.

4 Meanwhile, place the saffron strands in a small bowl. Add a boiling water and leave to soak.

5 Add the butter to the pan and stir in the saffron mixture. Cook gently for 10 minutes, or until the potatoes are tender.

6 Garnish the gingered potatoes with the celery leaves and serve at once.

COOK'S TIP

Use a nonstick, heavy-based skillet as the potato mixture is fairly dry and may stick to an ordinary pan.

VARIATION

If you prefer a less spicy dish, seed the chopped green chili or omit the chili altogether.

Thai Potato Stir-Fry

This dish has a traditional sweet-and-sour Thai flavoring. Tender vegetables are simply stir-fried with spices and coconut milk, and flavored with lime.

Serves 4

INGREDIENTS

4 waxy potatoes, diced
2 tbsp vegetable oil
1 yellow bell pepper, diced
1 red bell pepper, diced
1 carrot, cut into matchstick strips
1 zucchini, cut into matchstick strips

2 garlic cloves, crushed
1 red chili, sliced
1 bunch scallions, halved lengthwise
8 tbsp coconut milk
1 tsp chopped lemon grass
2 tsp lime juice

finely grated rind of 1 lime
1 tbsp chopped fresh cilantro

1 Cook the diced potatoes in a saucepan of boiling water for 5 minutes. Drain thoroughly.

2 Heat the oil in a wok or large skillet and add the potatoes, diced bell peppers, carrot, zucchini, garlic, and chili. Stir-fry the vegetables for 2–3 minutes.

3 Stir in the scallions, coconut milk, chopped lemon grass, and lime juice and stir-fry the mixture for a further 5 minutes.

4 Add the lime rind and cilantro and stir-fry for 1 minute. Serve hot.

COOK'S TIP

Check that the potatoes are not overcooked in step 1, otherwise the potato pieces will disintegrate when they are stir-fried in the wok.

VARIATION

Almost any combination of vegetables is suitable for this dish; the yellow and red bell peppers, for example, can be replaced with crisp green beans or snow peas.

Cheese & Potato Slices

This recipe takes a while to prepare, but it is well worth the effort. The golden potato slices coated in bread crumbs and cheese are delicious served with fish, or simply on their own.

Serves 4

INGREDIENTS

3 large waxy potatoes, unpeeled and thickly sliced	1/2 cup grated Parmesan cheese	oil, for deep frying
1 cup fresh white bread crumbs	1 1/2 tsp chili powder	chili powder, for dusting (optional)
	2 eggs, beaten	

1 Cook the sliced potatoes in a saucepan of boiling water for 10–15 minutes, or until the potatoes are just tender. Drain thoroughly.

2 Mix the bread crumbs, cheese, and chili powder together in a bowl then transfer to a shallow dish. Pour the beaten eggs into a separate shallow dish.

3 Dip the potato slices in egg and then roll them in the bread crumbs to coat completely.

4 Heat the oil in a large saucepan or deep-fryer to 350°F–375°F, or until a cube of bread browns in 30 seconds. Cook the cheese and potato slices, in several batches and turning occasionally, for 4–5 minutes, or until a golden brown color.

5 Remove the cheese and potato slices with a slotted spoon and leave to drain thoroughly on paper towels. Keep the cheese and potato slices warm while you cook the remaining batches.

6 Transfer the cheese and potato slices to warm serving plates. Dust with chili powder, if using, and serve immediately.

VARIATION

For a healthy alternative, use fresh whole-wheat bread crumbs instead of the white ones used here, if you prefer.

COOK'S TIP

The cheese and potato slices may be coated in the breadcrumb mixture in advance and then stored in the refrigerator until ready to use.

Broiled Potatoes with Lime Mayonnaise

This dish is ideal with broiled or barbecued foods, as the potatoes themselves may be cooked by either method.

Serves 4

INGREDIENTS

1 pound potatoes, unpeeled and
   scrubbed
3 tbsp butter, melted
2 tbsp chopped fresh thyme
paprika, for dusting

LIME MAYONNAISE:
$2/3$ cup mayonnaise
2 tsp lime juice
finely grated rind of 1 lime
1 garlic clove, crushed

pinch of paprika
salt and pepper

1 Cut the potatoes into $1/2$-inch thick slices.

2 Cook the potatoes in a saucepan of boiling water for 5–7 minutes—they should still be quite firm. Remove the potatoes with a slotted spoon and drain thoroughly.

3 Line a broiler pan with foil. Place the potato slices on top of the foil.

4 Brush the potatoes with the melted butter and sprinkle the chopped thyme on top. Season to taste with salt and pepper.

5 Cook the potatoes under a preheated broiler for 10 minutes, turning once.

6 Meanwhile, make the lime mayonnaise. Combine the mayonnaise, lime juice, lime rind, garlic, paprika, and salt and pepper to taste in a bowl.

7 Dust the hot potato slices with a little paprika and serve with the lime mayonnaise.

COOK'S TIP

For an impressive side dish, thread the potato slices onto skewers and cook over medium hot barbecue coals.

COOK'S TIP

The lime mayonnaise may be spooned over the broiled potatoes to coat them just before serving, if you prefer.

Trio of Potato Purées

These small molds filled with layers of flavored potato look very impressive when served for a special occasion. They are ideal with fish or roasts.

Serves 4

INGREDIENTS

10$\frac{1}{2}$ ounces mealy potatoes, chopped

4$\frac{1}{2}$ ounces rutabaga, chopped

1 carrot, chopped

1 pound spinach

1 tbsp milk

1 tbsp butter

$\frac{1}{4}$ cup all-purpose flour

1 egg

$\frac{1}{2}$ tsp ground cinnamon

1 tbsp orange juice

$\frac{1}{4}$ tsp grated nutmeg

salt and pepper

carrot matchsticks, to garnish

1 Lightly grease four $\frac{2}{3}$-cup ramekins or ovenproof mini pudding bowls

2 Cook the potatoes in a saucepan of boiling water for 10 minutes. Meanwhile, in separate pans, cook the rutabaga and carrot in boiling water for 10 minutes. Blanch the spinach in a little boiling water for 5 minutes. Drain all the vegetables.

3 Add the milk and butter to the potatoes and mash until smooth. Stir in the flour and egg.

4 Divide the potato mixture into 3 equal portions and place in 3 separate bowls. Spoon the rutabaga into one bowl and mix well. Spoon the carrot into the second bowl and mix well. Spoon the spinach into the third bowl and mix well.

5 Add the cinnamon to the rutabaga and potato mixture and season with salt and pepper to taste. Stir the orange juice into the carrot and potato mixture. Stir the nutmeg into the spinach and potato mixture.

6 Spoon a layer of the rutabaga and potato mixture into each of the ramekins or bowls and smooth the top. Cover each with a layer of spinach and potato mixture, then top with the carrot and potato mixture. Cover the ramekins with foil and place in a roasting pan. Half fill the pan with boiling water and cook in a preheated oven at 350°F for 40 minutes, or until set.

7 Turn out onto serving plates, garnish with the carrot matchsticks, and serve at once.

Spicy Potato Fries

These are home-made fries with a difference, flavored with spices and cooked in the oven. Serve with hamburgers or steak.

Serves 4

INGREDIENTS

4 large waxy potatoes
2 sweet potatoes

4 tbsp butter, melted
1/2 tsp chili powder

1 tsp garam masala
salt

1 Cut the potatoes and sweet potatoes into slices about 1/2 inch thick, then cut them into fries.

2 Place the potatoes in a large bowl of cold salted water. Soak for 20 minutes.

3 Remove the potato slices with a slotted spoon and drain thoroughly. Pat with paper towels until completely dry.

4 Pour the melted butter onto a cookie sheet. Transfer the potato slices to the cookie sheet. Sprinkle with the chili powder and garam masala, turning the potato slices to coat them thoroughly with the mixture.

5 Cook the fries in a preheated oven at 400°F for 40 minutes, turning frequently, until browned and cooked through.

6 Drain the fries on paper towels to remove the excess oil and serve at once.

COOK'S TIP

Rinsing the potatoes in cold water before cooking removes the starch, thus preventing them from sticking together. Soaking the potatoes in a bowl of cold salted water actually makes the cooked fries crisper.

VARIATION

For added flavor, sprinkle the fries with fennel seeds or cumin seeds, before serving.

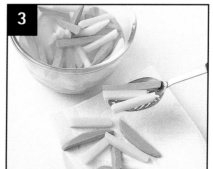

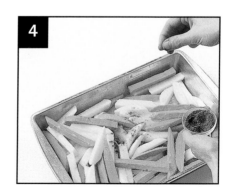

Italian Potato Wedges

These oven-cooked potato wedges use classic pizza ingredients and are delicious served with plain meats, such as pork or lamb.

Serves 4

INGREDIENTS

2 large waxy potatoes, unpeeled
4 large ripe tomatoes, skinned and seeded
$^2/_3$ cup vegetable stock

2 tbsp tomato paste
1 small yellow bell pepper, cut into strips
$1^1/_2$ cups button mushrooms, quartered

1 tbsp chopped fresh basil
$^1/_2$ cup grated cheese
salt and pepper

1 Cut each of the potatoes into 8 equal wedges. Parboil the potatoes in a pan of boiling water for 15 minutes. Drain well and place in a shallow ovenproof dish.

2 Chop the tomatoes and add to the dish. Mix together the vegetable stock and tomato paste, then pour the mixture on top of the potatoes and tomatoes.

3 Add the yellow bell pepper strips, quartered mushrooms, and chopped basil. Season well with salt and pepper.

4 Sprinkle the grated cheese over the top and cook in a preheated oven at 375°F for 15–20 minutes, until the topping is golden brown. Serve at once.

COOK'S TIP

For the topping, use any cheese that melts well, such as Mozzarella, the traditional pizza cheese. Alternatively, you could use Swiss cheese, if you prefer.

COOK'S TIP

These potato wedges can also be served as a light supper dish, accompanied by chunks of crusty, fresh brown or white bread.

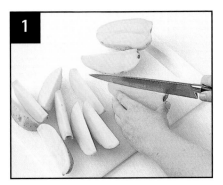

Saffron-flavored Potatoes with Mustard

Saffron is actually made from the dried stigma of the crocus and is native to Greece. It is very expensive, but only a very small amount is needed to flavor a dish.

Serves 4

INGREDIENTS

1 tsp saffron strands
6 tbsp boiling water
1¹/₂ pound waxy potatoes, unpeeled
 and cut into wedges
1 red onion, cut into 8 wedges

2 garlic cloves, crushed
1 tbsp white wine vinegar
2 tbsp olive oil
1 tbsp wholegrain mustard
5 tbsp vegetable stock

5 tbsp dry white wine
2 tsp chopped fresh rosemary
salt and pepper

1 Place the saffron strands in a small bowl and pour over the boiling water. Soak for about 10 minutes.

2 Place the potatoes in a roasting pan, together with the red onion wedges and crushed garlic.

3 Add the vinegar, oil, mustard, vegetable stock, white wine, rosemary, and saffron water to the potatoes and onion in the pan. Season to taste with salt and pepper.

4 Cover the roasting pan with foil and bake in a preheated oven at 400°F for 30 minutes.

5 Remove the foil and cook the potatoes for a further 10 minutes, until crisp, browned, and cooked through. Serve hot.

VARIATION

If preferred, use only wine to flavor the potatoes, rather than a mixture of wine and stock.

COOK'S TIP

Turmeric may be used instead of saffron to provide the yellow color in this recipe. However, it is worth using saffron, if possible, for the lovely nutty flavor it gives a dish.

Chili Roast Potatoes

A delicious variation of the traditional roast potato, here small new potatoes are scrubbed and boiled in their skins, before being coated in a chili mixture and roasted to perfection in the oven.

Serves 4

INGREDIENTS

1 pound small new potatoes,
  scrubbed
2/3 cup vegetable oil

1 tsp chili powder
1/2 tsp caraway seeds

1 tsp salt
1 tbsp chopped fresh basil

1 Cook the potatoes in a saucepan of boiling water for 10 minutes. Drain the potatoes thoroughly.

2 Pour a sufficient quantity of the oil into a shallow roasting pan to coat the base. Heat the oil in a preheated oven at 400°F for 10 minutes. Add the potatoes to the pan and brush them with the hot oil.

3 In a small bowl, mix together the chili powder, caraway seeds, and salt. Sprinkle the mixture over the potatoes, turning to coat them all over.

4 Add the remaining oil to the pan and roast in the oven for about 15 minutes, or until the potatoes are cooked through.

5 Using a slotted spoon, remove the potatoes from the the oil, and transfer them to a warm serving dish. Sprinkle the chopped basil over the top and serve immediately.

VARIATION

Use any other spice of your choice, such as curry powder or paprika, for a variation in flavor.

COOK'S TIP

Theses spicy potatoes are ideal for serving with plain meat dishes, such as roasted or broiled lamb, pork, or chicken.

Parmesan Potatoes

This is a very simple way to jazz up roast potatoes. Serve them in the same way as roast potatoes with roasted meat or fish.

Serves

INGREDIENTS

6 potatoes
$2/3$ cup grated Parmesan cheese
pinch of grated nutmeg

1 tbsp chopped fresh parsley
4 smoked bacon slices, cut into strips
oil, for roasting

salt

1 Cut the potatoes in half lengthwise and cook them in a saucepan of boiling salted water for 10 minutes. Drain thoroughly.

2 Mix the grated Parmesan cheese, nutmeg, and parsley together in a shallow bowl.

3 Roll the potato pieces in the cheese mixture to coat them completely. Shake off any excess.

4 Pour a little oil into a roasting pan and heat it in a preheated oven at 400°F for 10 minutes. Remove from the oven and place the potatoes into the pan. Return

the pa) to the oven and cook for 30 minutes, turning once.

5 Remove from the oven and sprinkle the bacon on top of the potatoes. Return to the oven for 15 minutes, or until the potatoes and bacon are cooked. Drain off any excess fat and serve.

COOK'S TIP

Parmesan cheese has been used for its distinctive flavor, but any finely grated hard cheese would be suitable for this dish.

VARIATION

If you prefer, use slices of salami or prosciutto instead of the bacon, adding it to the dish 5 minutes before the end of the cooking time.

Potatoes Dauphinois

This is a classic potato dish of layered potatoes, cream, garlic, onion, and cheese.
Serve with poached fish, such as fresh salmon, or smoked fish for a delicious meal.

Serves 4

INGREDIENTS

1 tbsp butter
1¹/2 pounds waxy potatoes, sliced
2 garlic cloves, crushed

1 red onion, sliced
3/4 cup grated Swiss cheese

1¹/4 cups heavy cream
salt and pepper

1 Lightly grease a 4-cup shallow ovenproof dish with a little butter.

2 Arrange a single layer of potato slices in the base of the prepared dish.

3 Top the potato slices with a little of the garlic, sliced red onion, and grated Swiss cheese. Season to taste with a little salt and pepper.

4 Repeat the layers in exactly the same order, finishing with a layer of potatoes topped with cheese.

5 Pour the cream over the top of the potatoes and cook in a preheated oven at 350°F for 1¹/2 hours, or until the potatoes are cooked through, browned, and crisp. Serve at once.

COOK'S TIP

There are many versions of this classic potato dish, but the different recipes always contain heavy cream, making it a rich and very filling side dish or accompaniment. This recipe must be cooked in a shallow dish to ensure there is plenty of crispy topping.

VARIATION

Add a layer of chopped bacon or ham to this dish, if desired, and serve with crisp salad greens for a light supper.

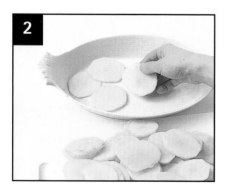

Pommes Anna

This is a classic potato dish, which may be left to cook unattended while the remainder of the meal is prepared, making it a suitable accompaniment to long-cooking casseroles or stews.

Serves 4

INGREDIENTS

¹/₄ cup butter, melted
1¹/₂ pounds waxy potatoes

4 tbsp chopped mixed fresh herbs
salt and pepper

chopped fresh herbs, to garnish

1 Brush a shallow 4-cup ovenproof dish with a little of the melted butter.

2 Slice the potatoes thinly and pat dry with paper towels.

3 Arrange a layer of potato slices in the prepared dish until the base is covered. Brush with a little butter and sprinkle with a quarter of the chopped mixed herbs. Season to taste.

4 Continue layering the potato slices, brushing each layer with melted butter and sprinkling with herbs, until all the potato slices are used up.

5 Brush the top layer of potato slices with butter, cover the dish, and cook in a preheated oven at 375°F for 1¹/₂ hours.

6 Turn out onto a warm ovenproof platter and return to the oven for a further 25–30 minutes, until golden brown. Serve at once, garnished with herbs.

COOK'S TIP

Make sure that the potatoes are sliced very thinly until they are almost transparent, in order that they cook thoroughly.

COOK'S TIP

The butter holds the potato slices together so that the cooked dish can be turned out. Therefore, it is important that the potato slices are dried thoroughly with paper towels before layering them in the dish, otherwise the butter will not be able to stick to them.

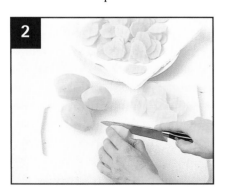

Potatoes with Almonds & Cream

This oven-cooked dish has a subtle creamy, almond flavor and a pale yellow color as a result of being cooked with turmeric.

Serves 4

INGREDIENTS

2 large potatoes, unpeeled and sliced	$^1/_2$ cup flaked almond	$4^1/_2$ ounces arugula
1 tbsp vegetable oil	$^1/_2$ tsp turmeric	salt and pepper
1 red onion, halved and sliced	$1^1/_4$ cups heavy cream	
1 garlic clove, crushed		

1 Cook the sliced potatoes in a saucepan of boiling water for 10 minutes. Drain thoroughly.

2 Heat the vegetable oil in a skillet and cook the onion and garlic for 3–4 minutes, stirring frequently.

3 Add the almonds, turmeric, and potato slices to the skillet and cook for 2–3 minutes, stirring constantly. Stir in the arugula.

4 Transfer the potato and almond mixture to a shallow ovenproof dish. Pour the heavy cream over the top and season with salt and pepper.

5 Cook in a preheated oven at 375°F for 20 minutes, or until the potatoes are cooked through. Serve as an accompaniment to broiled meat or fish dishes.

VARIATION

You could use other nuts, such as unsalted peanuts or cashews, instead of the almond flakes, if desired.

VARIATION

If arugula is unavailable, use the same quantity of trimmed baby spinach instead.

Casseroled Potatoes

This potato dish is cooked in the oven with leeks and wine.
It is very quick and simple to make.

Serves 4

INGREDIENTS

1¹/₂ pounds waxy potatoes, cut
  into chunks
1 tbsp butter
2 leeks, sliced
²/₃ cup dry white wine

²/₃ cup vegetable stock
1 tbsp lemon juice
2 tbsp chopped mixed fresh herbs
salt and pepper

TO GARNISH:
grated lemon rind
mixed fresh herbs (optional)

1 Cook the potato chunks in a saucepan of boiling water for 5 minutes. Drain thoroughly.

2 Meanwhile, melt the butter in a skillet and sauté the leeks for 5 minutes, or until they have softened.

3 Spoon the partly cooked potatoes and leeks into the base of an ovenproof dish.

4 Mix together the wine, vegetable stock, lemon juice, and chopped mixed herbs. Season to taste with salt and pepper, then pour the mixture over the potatoes.

5 Cook in a preheated oven at 375°F for 35 minutes, or until the potatoes are tender – to test, insert a sharp knife or skewer.

6 Garnish the potato casserole with lemon rind and fresh herbs, if using, and serve as an accompaniment to meat casseroles or roast meat.

COOK'S TIP

Cover the ovenproof dish halfway through cooking if the leeks start to brown on the top.

Cheese Crumble-Topped Mash

This is a delicious way to liven up mashed potato by topping it with a crumble mixture flavored with herbs, mustard, and onion, which turns crunchy on baking.

Serves 4

INGREDIENTS

2 pounds mealy potatoes, diced
2 tbsp butter
2 tbsp milk
1/2 cup grated sharp cheese or blue
   cheese

CRUMBLE TOPPING:
3 tbsp butter
1 onion, cut into chunks
1 garlic clove, crushed
1 tbsp wholegrain mustard

3 cups fresh whole-wheat
   bread crumbs
2 tbsp chopped fresh parsley
salt and pepper

1 Cook the potatoes in a pan of boiling water for 10 minutes, or until cooked through.

2 Meanwhile, make the crumble topping. Melt the butter in a skillet. Add the onion, garlic, and mustard and fry gently for 5 minutes, until the onion chunks have softened, stirring constantly.

3 Put the bread crumbs in a mixing bowl and stir in the fried onion. Season to taste with salt and pepper.

4 Drain the potatoes thoroughly and place them in a mixing bowl. Add the butter and milk, then mash until smooth. Stir in the grated cheese while the potato is still hot.

5 Spoon the mashed potato into a shallow ovenproof dish and sprinkle with the crumble topping.

6 Cook in a preheated oven at 400°F for 10–15 minutes, until the crumble topping is golden brown and crunchy. Serve immediately.

COOK'S TIP

For extra crunch, add freshly cooked vegetables, such as celery and bell peppers, to the mashed potato in step 4.

Carrot & Potato Soufflé

Hot soufflés have a reputation for being difficult to make, but this one is both simple and impressive. Make sure you serve the soufflé as soon as it is cooked.

Serves 4

INGREDIENTS

2 tbsp butter, melted
4 tbsp fresh whole-wheat
   bread crumbs

$1^1/_2$ pounds mealy potatoes, baked in
   their skins
2 carrots, grated
2 eggs, separated

2 tbsp orange juice
$^1/_4$ tsp grated nutmeg
salt and pepper
carrot curls, to garnish

1 Brush the inside of a $3^3/_4$-cup soufflé dish with butter. Sprinkle three-quarters of the bread crumbs over the base and sides of the dish.

2 Cut the baked potatoes in half and scoop the flesh into a mixing bowl.

3 Add the carrot, egg yolks, orange juice, and nutmeg to the potato flesh. Season to taste with salt and pepper.

4 In a separate bowl, beat the egg whites until they stand in soft peaks, then gently fold into the potato mixture with a metal spoon until well incorporated.

5 Gently spoon the potato and carrot mixture into the prepared soufflé dish. Sprinkle the remaining bread crumbs over the top of the mixture.

6 Cook in a preheated oven at 400°F/ for 40 minutes, until risen and golden. Do not open the oven door during the cooking time, otherwise the soufflé will sink. Serve at once, garnished with carrot curls.

COOK'S TIP

To bake the potatoes, prick the skins and cook in a preheated oven at 375°F for about 1 hour.

Side Dishes

Steamed Potatoes en Papillotes

New potatoes are just the right size for this method of cooking. The potatoes and vegetables are wrapped in waxed paper, sealed, and steamed in the oven.

Serves 4

INGREDIENTS

16 small new potatoes
1 carrot, cut into matchstick strips
1 fennel bulb, sliced

1 cup green beans
1 yellow bell pepper, cut into strips
16 tbsp dry white wine

4 rosemary sprigs
salt and pepper
rosemary sprigs, to garnish

1 Cut 4 squares of waxed paper measuring about 10 inches in size.

2 Divide the vegetables equally between the 4 paper squares, placing them in the center.

3 Bring the edges of the paper together and scrunch them together to encase the vegetables, leaving the top open.

4 Place the parcels in a shallow roasting pan and spoon 4 tbsp of white wine into each packet. Add a rosemary sprig and season with salt and pepper.

5 Fold the top of each packet over to seal it. Cook in a preheated oven at 375°F for 30–35 minutes, or until the vegetables are tender.

6 Transfer the sealed packets to 4 individual serving plates and garnish with rosemary sprigs. The packets should be opened at the table in order for the full aroma of the vegetables to be appreciated.

COOK'S TIP

These packets may be cooked in a steamer, if preferred.

VARIATION

If small new potatoes are unavailable, use larger potatoes which have been halved or quartered to ensure that they cook through in the specified cooking time.

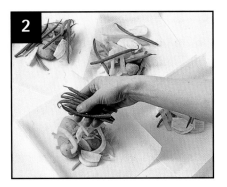
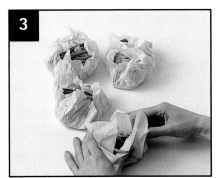

154

Main Meals

This chapter contains a wide selection of delicious main meal dishes which are more substantial than the snacks and light meals section and generally require more preparation and cooking. The potato is the main ingredient in the majority of the recipes in this chapter, but they also include ideas for adding meat, poultry, fish, and vegetarian ingredients—so that there is sure to be something for everyone.

The recipes come from all around the world— try Potato Ravioli, Potato & Lamb Kofta, Spanish Potato Bake, or Potato Curry. There are also lots of hearty and filling dishes, including Creamy Chicken & Potato Casserole, Four Cheese & Potato Layer Bake, and Potato & Eggplant Gratin. Whether you are cooking for one or two, a family, or a number of guests at a dinner party, you will find something here to entice you!

Potato, Beef, & Peanut Pot

The spicy peanut sauce in this recipe will complement almost any meat; although beef is used here, the dish is just as delicious made with chicken or pork.

Serves 4

INGREDIENTS

1 tbsp vegetable oil

1/4 cup butter

1 pound lean beef steak, cut into thin strips

1 onion, halved and sliced

2 garlic cloves, crushed

2 large waxy potatoes, cubed

1/2 tsp paprika

4 tbsp crunchy peanut butter

2 1/2 cups beef stock

1/4 cup unsalted peanuts

2 tsp light soy sauce

1 3/4 oz sugar snap peas

1 red bell pepper, cut into strips

parsley sprigs, to garnish (optional)

1 Heat the oil and butter in a flameproof casserole dish.

2 Add the beef strips and sauté them gently for 3–4 minutes, stirring and turning the meat, until it is sealed on all sides.

3 Add the onion and garlic and cook for a further 2 minutes, stirring constantly.

4 Add the potato cubes and cook for 3–4 minutes, or until they begin to brown slightly.

5 Stir in the paprika and peanut butter, then gradually blend in the beef stock. Bring the mixture to a boil, stirring frequently.

6 Finally, add the peanuts, soy sauce, sugar snap peas, and red bell pepper.

7 Cover and cook over a low heat for 45 minutes, or until the beef is cooked through.

8 Garnish the dish with parsley sprigs, if desired, and serve.

COOK'S TIP

Serve this dish with plain boiled rice or noodles, if desired.

VARIATION

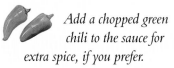
Add a chopped green chili to the sauce for extra spice, if you prefer.

Potato Ravioli

In this recipe the "pasta" dough is made with potatoes instead of the traditional flour. The small round ravioli are filled with a rich bolognese sauce and cooked in a skillet.

Serves 4

INGREDIENTS

FILLING:
1 tbsp vegetable oil
4^1/$_2$ ounces ground beef
1 shallot, diced
1 garlic clove, crushed
1 tbsp all-purpose flour
1 tbsp tomato paste
^{2}/$_3$ cup beef stock

1 celery stalk, chopped
2 tomatoes, skinned and diced
2 tsp chopped fresh basil
salt and pepper

RAVIOLI:
1 pound mealy potatoes, diced
3 small egg yolks

3 tbsp olive oil
1^1/$_2$ cups all-purpose flour
^{1}/$_4$ cup butter, for frying
shredded basil leaves, to garnish

1 To make the filling, heat the oil in a pan and fry the beef for 3–4 minutes, breaking it up with a spoon. Add the shallot and garlic and cook for 2–3 minutes, until the shallot has softened.

2 Stir in the flour and tomato paste and cook for 1 minute. Stir in the beef stock, celery, tomatoes, and chopped fresh basil. Season to taste with salt and pepper.

3 Cook the mixture over a low heat for 20 minutes. Remove from the heat and let cool.

4 To make the ravioli, cook the potatoes in a pan of boiling water for 10 minutes, until tender.

5 Mash the potatoes and place them in a mixing bowl. Blend in the egg yolks and oil. Season with salt and pepper, then stir in the flour and mix to form a dough.

6 On a lightly floured surface, divide the dough into 24 pieces and shape into flat rounds. Spoon the filling onto half of each round and fold the dough over to encase the filling, pressing down to seal the edges.

7 Melt the butter in a skillet and cook the ravioli for 6–8 minutes, turning once, until golden. Serve hot, garnished with shredded basil leaves.

Veal Italienne

This dish is really superb if made with tender veal. However, if veal is unavailable, use pork or turkey fillets instead.

Serves 4

INGREDIENTS

$^{1}/_{4}$ cup butter
1 tbsp olive oil
$1^{1}/_{2}$ pounds potatoes, cubed
4 veal escalopes, weighing about 6 ounces each
1 onion, cut into 8 wedges
2 garlic cloves, crushed

2 tbsp all-purpose flour
2 tbsp tomato paste
$^{2}/_{3}$ cup red wine
$1^{1}/_{4}$ cups chicken stock
8 ripe tomatoes, skinned, seeded, and diced

$^{1}/_{4}$ cup pitted black olives, halved
2 tbsp chopped fresh basil
salt and pepper
fresh basil leaves, to garnish

1 Heat the butter and oil in a large skillet. Add the potato cubes and cook for 5–7 minutes, stirring frequently, until they begin to brown.

2 Remove the potatoes from the skillet with a slotted spoon and set aside.

3 Place the veal in the skillet and cook for 2–3 minutes on each side, until sealed. Remove from the pan and set aside.

4 Stir the onion and garlic into the skillet and cook for 2–3 minutes.

5 Add the flour and tomato paste and cook for 1 minute, stirring. Gradually blend in the red wine and chicken stock, stirring to make a smooth sauce.

6 Return the potatoes and veal to the skillet. Stir in the tomatoes, olives, and chopped basil and season with salt and pepper.

7 Transfer to a casserole dish and cook in a preheated oven at 350°F for 1 hour, or until the potatoes and veal are cooked through. Garnish with basil leaves and serve.

COOK'S TIP

For a quicker cooking time and really tender meat, pound the meat with a meat mallet to flatten it slightly before cooking.

Lamb Hot-Pot

No potato cookbook would be complete without this classic recipe using lamb cutlets layered between sliced potatoes, kidneys, onions, and herbs.

Serves 4

INGREDIENTS

1$^{1}/_{2}$ pounds rack of lamb cutlets
2 lamb's kidneys
1$^{1}/_{2}$ pounds waxy potatoes, scrubbed
   and thinly sliced

1 large onion, sliced thinly
2 tbsp chopped fresh thyme
$^{2}/_{3}$ cup lamb stock
2 tbsp butter, melted

salt and pepper
fresh thyme sprigs, to garnish

1 Remove any excess fat from the lamb. Skin and core the kidneys, and cut them into slices.

2 Arrange a layer of potatoes in the base of a 7$^{1}/_{2}$-cup ovenproof dish.

3 Arrange the lamb cutlets on top of the potatoes and cover with the sliced kidneys, onion, and chopped fresh thyme.

4 Pour the lamb stock over the meat and season to taste with salt and pepper.

5 Layer the remaining potato slices on top, overlapping to completely cover the meat and sliced onion.

6 Brush the potato slices with the butter, cover the dish and cook in a preheated oven at 350°F for 1$^{1}/_{2}$ hours.

7 Remove the lid and cook for a further 30 minutes, until golden brown on top.

8 Garnish with fresh thyme sprigs and serve hot.

COOK'S TIP

Although this is a classic recipe, extra ingredients of your choice, such as celery or carrots, can be added to the dish for variety and color.

VARIATION

Traditionally, oysters are also included in this tasty hot-pot. Add them to the layers along with the kidneys, if desired.

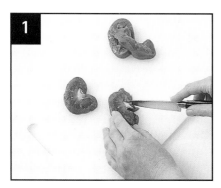

Potato & Lamb Kofta

Kofta is a Greek dish which is traditionally served threaded onto a skewer.
Here the kofta *are served on a plate with a refreshing* tzatziki *sauce.*

Serves 4

INGREDIENTS

1 pound mealy potatoes, diced
2 tbsp butter
8 ounces ground lamb
1 onion, chopped
2 garlic cloves, crushed

$^1/_2$ tsp ground coriander
2 eggs, beaten
oil, for deep-frying
mint sprigs, to garnish

SAUCE:
$^2/_3$ cup unsweetened yogurt
2 ounces cucumber, finely chopped
1 tbsp chopped mint
1 garlic clove, crushed

1 Cook the diced potatoes in a saucepan of boiling water for 10 minutes, until cooked through. Drain, mash until smooth, and transfer to a mixing bowl.

2 Melt the butter in a skillet, add the lamb, onion, garlic, and coriander and fry for 15 minutes, stirring.

3 Drain off the liquid from the skillet, then stir the meat mixture into the mashed potatoes. Stir in the eggs and season.

4 To make the sauce, combine the yogurt, cucumber, mint, and garlic in a bowl and set aside.

5 Heat the oil in a large saucepan or a deep-fryer to 350°F–375°F, or until a cube of bread browns in 30 seconds. Drop spoonfuls of the potato mixture into the hot oil and cook in batches for 4–5 minutes, or until golden brown.

6 Remove the *kofta* with a slotted spoon, drain

thoroughly on paper towels, set aside, and keep warm. Garnish with fresh mint sprigs and serve with the sauce.

COOK'S TIP

These kofta can be made with any sort of ground meat, such as turkey, chicken, or pork, and flavored with appropriate fresh herbs, such as sage or cilantro.

Spanish Potato Bake

This is a variation of a traditional Spanish dish, Huevos, where eggs are served on top of a tomato mixture. Here eggs are cooked on top of a spicy sausage, tomato, and potato mixture.

Serves 4

INGREDIENTS

1¹/₂ pounds waxy potatoes, diced
3 tbsp olive oil
1 onion, halved and sliced
2 garlic cloves, crushed
14 ounce can plum tomatoes, chopped

2³/₄ ounces chorizo sausage, sliced
1 green bell pepper, cut into strips
¹/₂ tsp paprika
¹/₄ cup pitted black olives, halved
8 eggs

1 tbsp chopped fresh parsley
salt and pepper

1 Cook the diced potatoes in a saucepan of boiling water for 10 minutes, or until softened. Drain and set aside.

2 Heat the olive oil in a skillet, add the onion and garlic, and fry gently for 2–3 minutes, until the onion softens.

3 Add the chopped canned tomatoes and cook over a low heat for about 10 minutes, or until the mixture has reduced slightly.

4 Stir the potatoes into the skillet with the chorizo, bell pepper, paprika, and olives. Cook for 5 minutes, stirring. Transfer to a shallow ovenproof dish.

5 Make 8 small hollows in the top of the mixture and break an egg into each hollow.

6 Cook in a preheated oven at 425°F for 5–6 minutes, or until the eggs are just cooked. Sprinkle with parsley and serve with crusty bread.

VARIATION

Add a little spice to the dish by incorporating 1 tsp chili powder in step 4, if desired.

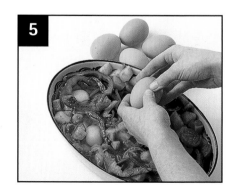

Potato & Pepperoni Pizza

Potatoes make a great pizza base and this recipe is well worth making, rather than using a ready-made base, both for texture and flavor.

Makes 1 large pizza

INGREDIENTS

2 pounds mealy potatoes, diced
1 tbsp butter
2 garlic cloves, crushed
2 tbsp mixed chopped fresh herbs
1 egg, beaten

$^1/_3$ cup sieved tomatoes
2 tbsp tomato paste
$^1/_2$ cup pepperoni slices
1 green bell pepper, cut into strips
1 yellow bell pepper, cut into strips

2 large open-cap mushrooms, sliced
$^1/_4$ cup pitted black olives, quartered
$4^1/_2$ ounces mozzarella cheese, sliced

1 Grease and flour a 9-inch pizza pan.

2 Cook the diced potatoes in a saucepan of boiling water for 10 minutes, or until cooked through. Drain and mash until smooth. Transfer the mashed potato to a mixing bowl and stir in the butter, garlic, herbs, and egg.

3 Spread the mixture into the prepared pizza pan. Cook in a preheated oven at 425°F for 7–10 minutes, or until the pizza base begins to set.

4 Mix the sieved tomatoes and tomato paste together and spoon it over the pizza base, to within $^1/_2$ inch of the edge.

5 Arrange the pepperoni, bell peppers, mushrooms, and olives on top of the sieved tomatoes.

6 Scatter the mozzarella cheese on top of the pizza. Cook in the oven for 20 minutes, or until the base is cooked through and the cheese has melted on top. Serve hot with a mixed salad.

COOK'S TIP

This pizza base is softer in texture than a normal bread dough and is ideal served from the pan. Top with any of your favorite pizza ingredients that you have to hand.

Potato & Sausage Panfry

This dish is a meal in itself, containing both meat and the potatoes cooked in
a herbed wine gravy. A selection of fresh vegetables may be served with the dish, if desired.

Serves 4

INGREDIENTS

1¹/₂ pounds waxy potatoes, cubed
2 tbsp butter
8 large herbed sausages
4 smoked bacon slices

1 onion, quartered
1 zucchini, sliced
²/₃ cup dry white wine
1¹/₄ cups vegetable stock

1 tsp Worcestershire sauce
2 tbsp chopped mixed fresh herbs
salt and pepper
chopped fresh herbs, to garnish

1 Cook the cubed potatoes in a saucepan of boiling water for 10 minutes, or until softened. Drain thoroughly and set aside.

2 Meanwhile, melt the butter in a large skillet. Add the herbed sausages and cook for 5 minutes, turning them frequently to ensure that they brown on all sides.

3 Add the bacon slices, onion, zucchini, and potatoes to the skillet. Cook the mixture for a further 10 minutes, stirring the mixture and turning the sausages frequently.

4 Stir in the white wine, stock, Worcestershire sauce, and chopped mixed herbs. Season with salt and pepper to taste and cook the mixture over a gentle heat for 10 minutes. Season with a little more salt and pepper, if necessary.

5 Transfer the potato and sausage panfry to warm serving plates, garnish with chopped fresh herbs, and serve at once.

COOK'S TIP

Use different flavors of sausage to vary the dish—there are many different varieties available, such as leek and mustard.

VARIATION

For an attractive color, use a red onion cut into quarters rather than a white onion.

Potato, Tomato, & Sausage Panfry

This is a very simple dish which is delicious as a main meal. Choose good sausages flavored either with herbs or use one of the many types of flavored sausages, such as mustard or leek.

Serves 4

INGREDIENTS

2 large potatoes, sliced
1 tbsp vegetable oil
8 flavored sausages
1 red onion, cut into 8
1 tbsp tomato paste

²/₃ cup red wine
²/₃ cup sieved tomatoes
2 large tomatoes, each cut into 8
6 ounces broccoli flowerets, blanched

2 tbsp chopped fresh basil
salt and pepper
shredded fresh basil, to garnish

1 Cook the sliced potatoes in a saucepan of boiling water for 7 minutes. Drain thoroughly and set aside.

2 Meanwhile, heat the oil in a large skillet. Add the sausages and cook for 5 minutes, turning the sausages frequently to ensure that they are browned on all sides.

3 Add the onion pieces to the pan and continue to cook for a further 5 minutes, stirring the mixture frequently.

4 Stir in the tomato paste, red wine, and the sieved tomatoes and mix together well. Add the tomato wedges, broccoli flowerets, and chopped basil to the panfry and mix carefully.

5 Add the parboiled potato slices to the pan. Cook the mixture for about 10 minutes, or until the sausages are completely cooked through. Season to taste with salt and pepper.

6 Garnish the panfry with fresh shredded basil and serve hot.

VARIATION

Broccoli is particularly good in this dish as it adds a splash of color, but other vegetables of your choice can be used instead, if preferred.

COOK'S TIP

Omit the sieved tomatoes from this recipe and use canned plum tomatoes or chopped tomatoes for convenience.

Potato, Chicken, & Banana Patties

Potato patties are a great favorite, but are usually served plain as a side dish. In this recipe, the potatoes are combined with ground chicken and mashed banana for a fruit-flavored main course.

Serves 4

INGREDIENTS

1 pound mealy potatoes, diced	1 onion, finely chopped	$^2/_3$ cup light cream
8 ounces ground chicken	2 tbsp chopped fresh sage	$^2/_3$ cup chicken stock
1 large banana	2 tbsp butter	salt and pepper
2 tbsp all-purpose flour	2 tbsp vegetable oil	fresh sage leaves, to garnish
1 tsp lemon juice		

1 Cook the diced potatoes in a saucepan of boiling water for 10 minutes, until cooked through. Drain and mash the potatoes until smooth. Stir in the chicken.

2 Mash the banana and add it to the potato with the flour, lemon juice, onion, and half the chopped sage. Season well and stir the mixture together.

3 Divide the mixture into 8 equal portions. With lightly floured hands, shape each portion into a round patty.

4 Heat the butter and oil in a skillet, add the potato patties and cook for 12–15 minutes, or until cooked through, turning once. Remove from the skillet and keep warm.

5 Stir the cream and stock into the skillet with the remaining chopped sage. Cook over a low heat for 2–3 minutes.

6 Arrange the potato patties on a serving plate, garnish with fresh sage leaves, and serve with the cream and sage sauce.

COOK'S TIP

Do not boil the sauce once the cream has been added, as it will curdle. Cook it gently over a very low heat.

Creamy Chicken & Potato Casserole

Small new potatoes are ideal for this recipe as they can be cooked whole. If larger potatoes are used, cut them in half or into chunks before adding them to the casserole.

Serves 4

INGREDIENTS

2 tbsp vegetable oil
$^{1}/_{4}$ cup butter
4 chicken portions, about 8 ounces each
2 leeks, sliced
1 garlic clove, crushed
4 tbsp all-purpose flour

$3^{3}/_{4}$ cups chicken stock
$1^{1}/_{4}$ cups dry white wine
$^{2}/_{3}$ cup baby carrots, halved lengthwise
$^{2}/_{3}$ cup baby corn cobs, halved lengthwise
1 pound small new potatoes

1 bouquet garni
$^{2}/_{3}$ cup heavy cream
salt and pepper

1 Heat the oil in a large skillet. Cook the chicken for 10 minutes, turning until browned all over. Transfer the chicken to a casserole dish using a slotted spoon.

2 Add the leek and garlic to the skillet and cook for 2–3 minutes, stirring. Stir in the flour and cook for a further 1 minute. Remove the skillet from the heat and stir in the stock and wine. Season well.

3 Return the skillet to the heat and bring the mixture to a boil. Stir in the carrots, corn, potatoes and bouquet garni.

4 Transfer the mixture to the casserole dish. Cover and cook in a preheated oven at 350°F for about 1 hour.

5 Remove the casserole from the oven and stir in the cream. Return the casserole to the oven, uncovered, and cook for a further 15 minutes. Remove the bouquet garni and discard. Taste and adjust the seasoning, if necessary. Serve the casserole with plain rice or fresh vegetables, such as broccoli or green beans.

COOK'S TIP

Use turkey fillets instead of the chicken, if desired, and vary the vegetables according to those you have to hand.

Potato-topped Cod

This simple dish has a spicy bread-crumb mixture topping layers of cod and potatoes. It is cooked in the oven until crisp and golden.

Serves 4

INGREDIENTS

¼ cup butter
4 waxy potatoes, sliced
1 large onion, finely chopped
1 tsp wholegrain mustard
1 tsp garam masala

pinch of chili powder
1 tbsp chopped fresh dill
1¼ cups fresh bread crumbs
4 cod fillets, about 6 ounces each
½ cup grated Swiss cheese

salt and pepper
fresh dill sprigs, to garnish

1 Melt half the butter in a skillet. Add the potatoes and fry for 5 minutes, turning until they are browned all over. Remove the potatoes from the skillet with a slotted spoon.

2 Add the remaining butter to the skillet and stir in the onion, mustard, garam masala, chili powder, chopped dill, and bread crumbs. Cook for 1–2 minutes, stirring well.

3 Layer half the potatoes in the base of an ovenproof dish and place the cod fillets on top. Cover the cod fillets with the rest of the potato slices. Season to taste with salt and pepper.

4 Spoon the spicy mixture from the skillet over the potatoes and sprinkle with the grated Swiss cheese.

5 Cook in a preheated oven at 400°F for 20–25 minutes, or until the topping is golden and crisp and the fish is cooked through. Garnish with fresh dill sprigs and serve at once.

VARIATION

You can use any fish for this recipe: for special occasions use salmon steaks or fillets.

COOK'S TIP

This dish is ideal served with baked vegetables which can be cooked in the oven at the same time.

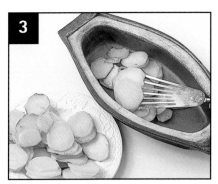

Potato Curry

Very little meat is eaten in India, their diet being mainly vegetarian. This potato curry with added vegetables makes a very substantial main meal.

Serves 4

INGREDIENTS

4 tbsp vegetable oil
1^1/$_2$ pound waxy potatoes, cut into
   large chunks
2 onions, quartered
3 garlic cloves, crushed
1 tsp garam masala
^{1}/$_2$ tsp turmeric

^{1}/$_2$ tsp ground cumin
^{1}/$_2$ tsp ground coriander
1-inch piece fresh ginger root, grated
1 red chili, chopped
8 ounces cauliflower flowerets
4 tomatoes, peeled and quartered
^{3}/$_4$ cup frozen peas

2 tbsp chopped fresh cilantro
1^1/$_4$ cups vegetable stock
shredded fresh cilantro, to garnish

1 Heat the vegetable oil in a large heavy-based saucepan or skillet. Add the potato chunks, onion, and garlic and fry gently for 2–3 minutes, stirring the mixture frequently.

2 Add the garam masala, turmeric, ground cumin, ground coriander, grated ginger, and chopped chili to the pan, mixing the spices into the vegetables. Fry for 1 minute, stirring constantly.

3 Add the cauliflower flowerets, tomatoes, peas, chopped cilantro, and vegetable stock to the curry mixture.

4 Cook the potato curry over a low heat for 30–40 minutes, or until the potatoes are completely cooked through.

5 Garnish the potato curry with fresh cilantro and serve with plain boiled rice or warm Indian bread.

COOK'S TIP

Use a large heavy-based saucepan or skillet for this recipe to ensure that the potatoes are cooked thoroughly.

Potato & Spinach Gnocchi

These small potato dumplings are flavored with spinach, cooked in boiling water, and served with a simple tomato sauce for an appetizing meal.

Serves 4

INGREDIENTS

10¹/₂ ounces mealy potatoes, diced
6 ounces spinach
1 egg yolk
1 tsp olive oil

1 cup all-purpose flour
salt and pepper
spinach leaves, to garnish

SAUCE:
1 tbsp olive oil
2 shallots, chopped
1 garlic clove, crushed
1¹/₄ cups sieved tomatoes
2 tsp soft light brown sugar

1 Cook the diced potatoes in a saucepan of boiling water for 10 minutes, until cooked through. Drain and mash the potatoes.

2 Meanwhile, in a separate pan, blanch the spinach in a little boiling water for 1–2 minutes. Drain well and shred the leaves.

3 Transfer the mashed potato to a lightly floured chopping board and make a well in the center. Add the egg yolk, olive oil, spinach, and a little of the flour and quickly mix the ingredients into the potato, adding more flour as you go, until you have a firm dough. Divide the mixture into very small dumplings.

4 Cook the gnocchi in batches in a saucepan of boiling salted water for about 5 minutes, or until they rise to the top of the pan.

5 Meanwhile, make the sauce. Put the oil, shallots, garlic, sieved tomatoes, and sugar into a saucepan and cook over a low heat for 10–15 minutes, or until the sauce has thickened.

6 Drain the gnocchi using a slotted spoon and transfer to warm serving dishes. Spoon the sauce over the gnocchi and garnish with the fresh spinach leaves.

VARIATION

Add chopped fresh herbs and cheese to the gnocchi dough instead of the spinach, if desired.

Potato-topped Vegetables in Wine

This is a very colorful and nutritious dish, packed full of crunchy vegetables in a wine sauce.
It may be made in one large dish or divided up into four individual pie dishes.

Serves 4

INGREDIENTS

1 carrot, diced	$^2/_3$ cup vegetable stock	TOPPING:
6 ounces cauliflower flowerets	$1^2/_3$ cup dry white wine	4 mealy potatoes, diced
6 ounces broccoli flowerets	$^2/_3$ cup milk	2 tbsp butter
1 fennel bulb, sliced	2 tbsp chopped fresh sage	4 tbsp unsweetened yogurt
$^3/_4$ cup green beans, halved	$2^1/_4$ cups quartered crimini	4 tbsp grated Parmesan cheese
2 tbsp butter	mushrooms	1 tsp fennel seeds
$^1/_4$ cup all-purpose flour		salt and pepper

1 Cook the carrot, cauliflower, broccoli, fennel, and beans in a saucepan of boiling water for 10 minutes. Drain the vegetables thoroughly and set aside.

2 Melt the butter in a saucepan and stir in the flour. Cook for 1 minute, then remove from the heat. Stir in the stock, wine, and milk and bring to a boil, stirring until thickened. Stir in the reserved vegetables and mushrooms.

3 Meanwhile, make the topping. Cook the diced potatoes in a separate pan of boiling water for 10–15 minutes, or until cooked through. Drain the potatoes and mash with the butter, yogurt, and half the cheese. Stir in the fennel seeds.

4 Spoon the vegetable mixture into a 4-cup pie dish. Spoon or pipe the potato on top, covering the filling completely. Sprinkle the remaining cheese on top. Cook in a preheated oven at 375°F for 30–35 minutes, or until the topping is golden. Serve hot.

COOK'S TIP

Any combination of vegetables may be used in this dish, and frozen mixed vegetables can be thawed and used for convenience and speed.

Potato & Three Cheese Soufflé

This is soufflé is very simple to make, yet it has a delicious flavor and melts in your mouth. Choose three alternative cheeses, if preferred, but make sure that they are all strongly flavored.

Serves 4

INGREDIENTS

2 tbsp butter
2 tsp all-purpose flour
2 pounds mealy potatoes

8 eggs, separated
$^{1}/_{4}$ cup grated Swiss cheese
$^{1}/_{4}$ cup crumbled blue cheese

$^{1}/_{4}$ cup grated sharp cheese
salt and pepper

1 Grease a 10-cup soufflé dish with the butter and dust with the flour. Set aside.

2 Cook the potatoes in a saucepan of boiling water until cooked through. Mash until very smooth and transfer to a mixing bowl to cool.

3 Beat the egg yolks into the potato and stir in the 3 different cheeses. Season well with salt and pepper.

4 In a clean bowl, beat the egg whites until standing in peaks, then gently fold them into the potato mixture with a metal spoon until fully incorporated.

5 Spoon the potato mixture into the prepared soufflé dish.

6 Cook in a preheated oven at 425°F for 35–40 minutes, until risen and set. Serve immediately.

COOK'S TIP

Insert a toothpick into the center of the soufflé; it should come out clean when the soufflé is fully cooked through.

VARIATION

You can add chopped cooked bacon to the soufflé for extra flavor, if desired.

Nutty Harvest Loaf

This vegetarian loaf is so delicious, that meat eaters will dig in without hesitation and not miss the meat! Served with a fresh tomato sauce, it can be eaten hot or cold with salad.

Serves 4

INGREDIENTS

1 pound mealy potatoes, diced
2 tbsp butter
1 onion, chopped
2 garlic cloves, crushed
³/₄ cup unsalted peanuts
1¹/₄ cups fresh white bread crumbs

1 egg, beaten
2 tbsp chopped fresh cilantro
²/₃ cup vegetable stock
1 cup closed-cap mushrooms, sliced
1 cup sliced sun-dried tomatoes
salt and pepper

SAUCE:
²/₃ cup crème fraîche
2 tsp tomato paste
2 tsp clear honey
2 tbsp chopped fresh cilantro

1 Grease a 1-pound loaf pan. Cook the potatoes in a saucepan of boiling water for 10 minutes, until cooked through. Drain well, mash, and set aside.

2 Melt half the butter in a skillet. Add the onion and garlic and sauté gently for 2–3 minutes, until soft. Finely chop the nuts or blend them in a food processor for 30 seconds with the bread crumbs.

3 Mix the chopped nuts and bread crumbs into the potatoes with the egg, cilantro, and vegetable stock. Stir in the onion and garlic and mix well.

4 Melt the remaining butter in the skillet, add the sliced mushrooms, and cook for 2–3 minutes.

5 Press half the potato mixture into the base of the loaf pan.

Spoon the mushrooms on top and sprinkle with the sun-dried tomatoes. Spoon the remaining potato mixture on top and smooth the surface. Cover with foil and bake in a preheated oven at 350°F for 1 hour, or until firm to the touch.

6 Meanwhile, mix the sauce ingredients together. Cut the nutty harvest loaf into slices and serve with the sauce.

Vegetable Cake

This is a savory version of a cheesecake with a layer of fried potatoes as a delicious base.
Thaw frozen mixed vegetables for the topping, if desired.

Serves 4

INGREDIENTS

BASE:
2 tbsp vegetable oil
4 large waxy potatoes, sliced thinly

TOPPING:
1 tbsp vegetable oil

1 leek, chopped
1 zucchini, grated
1 red bell pepper, diced
1 green bell pepper, diced
1 carrot, grated
2 tsp chopped fresh parsley

8 ounces full-fat soft cheese
$1/4$ cup grated sharp cheese
2 eggs, beaten
salt and pepper
shredded cooked leek, to garnish

1 Grease an 8-inch springform cake pan.

2 To make the base, heat the oil in a skillet. Cook the potato slices in batches over a medium heat until softened and browned. Drain thoroughly on paper towels and arrange the slices in the base of the pan.

3 To make the topping, heat the oil in a separate skillet and fry the leek over a low heat for 3–4 minutes, until softened.

4 Add the zucchini, bell peppers, carrot, and parsley to the skillet and cook over a low heat for 5–7 minutes, or until the vegetables have softened.

5 Meanwhile, beat the cheeses and eggs together in a bowl. Stir in the vegetables and season to taste with salt and pepper. Spoon the mixture on to the potato base.

6 Cook in a preheated oven at 375°F for 20–25 minutes, until the cake is set.

7 Remove the vegetable cake from the pan, garnish with shredded leek, and serve with a crisp salad.

COOK'S TIP

Add diced bean curd or diced meat, such as pork or chicken, to the topping, if desired. Cook the meat with the vegetables in step 4.

Bubble & Squeak

Bubble and squeak is best known as mashed potato and leftover green vegetables cooked in meat fat in a pan, and served as an accompaniment.

Serves 4

INGREDIENTS

1 pound mealy potatoes, diced
8 ounces Savoy cabbage, shredded
5 tbsp vegetable oil

2 leeks, chopped
1 garlic clove, crushed
8 ounces smoked bean curd, cubed

salt and pepper
shredded cooked leek, to garnish

1 Cook the diced potatoes in a saucepan of boiling water for 10 minutes, until tender. Drain and mash the potatoes.

2 Meanwhile, in a separate saucepan, blanch the cabbage in boiling water for 5 minutes. Drain and add to the potato.

3 Heat the oil in a heavy-based skillet, add the leeks and garlic, and sauté gently for 2–3 minutes. Stir into the potato and cabbage mixture.

4 Add the smoked bean curd and season well with salt and pepper. Cook over a moderate heat for 10 minutes.

5 Carefully turn the whole mixture over and continue to cook over a moderate heat for a further 5–7 minutes, until crispy underneath. Serve immediately, garnished with shredded leek.

COOK'S TIP

This vegetarian recipe is a perfect main meal, as the smoked bean curd cubes added to the basic bubble and squeak mixture make it very substantial.

VARIATION

You can add cooked meats, such as beef or chicken, instead of the bean curd for a more traditional recipe. Any gravy from the cooked meats can also be added, but ensure that the mixture is not too wet.

Potato Hash

This is a variation of the well-known dish, beef hash, which was made with salt beef and leftovers, and served to seagoing New Englanders.

Serves 4

INGREDIENTS

2 tbsp butter
1 red onion, halved and sliced
1 carrot, diced
^{1}/$_3$ cup green beans, halved

3 large waxy potatoes, diced
2 tbsp all-purpose flour
1^1/$_4$ cups vegetable stock
8 ounces bean curd, diced

salt and pepper
chopped fresh parsley, to garnish

1 Melt the butter in a skillet. Add the onion, carrot, green beans, and potatoes and sauté gently, stirring, for 5–7 minutes, or until the vegetables begin to brown.

2 Add the flour to the skillet and cook for 1 minute, stirring constantly. Gradually pour in the stock.

3 Reduce the heat and leave the mixture to simmer for 15 minutes, or until the potatoes are tender.

4 Add the diced bean curd to the mixture and cook for a further 5 minutes. Season to taste with salt and pepper.

5 Sprinkle the chopped parsley over the top of the potato hash to garnish, then serve hot straight from the skillet.

VARIATION

Use cooked diced meat, such as beef or lamb, instead of the bean curd for a nonvegetarian dish.

COOK'S TIP

Hash is a cooking term meaning to chop food into small pieces. Therefore a traditional hash dish is made from chopped fresh ingredients, such as roast beef or corned beef, bell peppers, onion, and celery, often served with gravy.

Twice Baked Potatoes with Pesto

This is an easy but very filling meal. The potatoes are baked until fluffy, then the flesh is scooped out and mixed with a tasty pesto filling before being returned to the potato shells and baked again.

Serves 4

INGREDIENTS

4 baking potatoes, about 8 ounces each

²/₃ cup heavy cream

¹/₃ cup vegetable stock

1 tbsp lemon juice

2 garlic cloves, crushed

3 tbsp chopped fresh basil

2 tbsp pine nuts

2 tbsp grated Parmesan cheese

salt and pepper

1 Scrub the potatoes and prick the skins with a fork. Rub a little salt into the skins and place on a cookie sheet.

2 Cook in a preheated oven at 375°F, for 1 hour or until the potatoes are cooked through and the skins crisp.

3 Remove the potatoes from the oven and cut them in half lengthwise. Using a spoon, scoop the potato flesh into a mixing bowl, leaving a thin shell of potato inside the skins. Mash the potato flesh with a fork.

4 Meanwhile, mix the cream and stock in a saucepan and simmer for 8–10 minutes, or until reduced by half.

5 Stir in the lemon juice, garlic, and chopped basil and season to taste with salt and pepper. Stir the mixture into the potato flesh with the pine nuts.

6 Spoon the mixture back into the potato shells and sprinkle the Parmesan cheese on top. Return the potatoes to the oven for 10 minutes, or until the cheese has browned. Serve with salad.

VARIATION

Add full-fat soft cheese or thinly sliced mushrooms to the mashed potato flesh in step 5, if you prefer.

Baked Potatoes with Guacamole & Salsa

This is a great way to eat a baked potato! Once cooked, the flesh is flavored with avocado and piled back into the shell with a salad garnish. It is then served with a hot tomato salsa.

Serves 4

INGREDIENTS

4 baking potatoes, about 8 ounces
  each
1 large ripe avocado
6 ounces smoked bean curd) diced
2 garlic cloves, crushed
1 onion, chopped finely

1 tomato, chopped finely
1 tsp lemon juice
4¹/₂ ounces mixed salad greens
fresh cilantro sprigs, to garnish

SALSA:
2 ripe tomatoes, seeded and diced
1 tbsp chopped cilantro
1 shallot, finely diced
1 green chili, diced
1 tbsp lemon juice
salt and pepper

1 Scrub the potatoes and prick the skins with a fork. Rub a little salt into the skins and place them on a cookie sheet.

2 Cook in a preheated oven at 375°F for 1 hour, or until cooked through and the skins are crisp.

3 Cut the potatoes in half lengthwise and scoop the flesh into a bowl, leaving a thin layer of potato inside the shells.

4 Halve and pit the avocado. Using a spoon, scoop out the avocado flesh and add to the bowl containing the potato. Stir in the lemon juice and mash the mixture together with a fork. Mix in the bean curd, garlic, onion, and tomato. Spoon the mixture into one half of the potato shells.

5 Arrange the salad greens on top of the guacamole mixture and place the other half of the potato shell on top.

6 To make the salsa, mix the tomatoes, cilantro, shallots, chili, lemon juice, and salt and pepper to taste in a bowl. Garnish the potatoes with sprigs of fresh cilantro and serve with the hot tomato salsa.

Pan Potato Cake

This tasty meal is made with sliced potatoes, bean curd, and vegetables cooked in the skillet from which it is served, and requires no accompaniment.

Serves 4

INGREDIENTS

1¹/₂ pounds waxy potatoes, unpeeled and sliced
1 carrot, diced
8 ounces small broccoli flowerets
¹/₄ cup butter

2 tbsp vegetable oil
1 red onion, quartered
2 garlic cloves, crushed
6 ounces bean curd, diced

2 tbsp chopped fresh sage
³/₄ cup grated sharp cheese

1 Cook the sliced potatoes in a saucepan of boiling water for 10 minutes. Drain thoroughly.

2 Meanwhile, cook the carrot and broccoli in a separate pan of boiling water for 5 minutes. Drain with a slotted spoon.

3 Heat the butter and oil in a 9-inch skillet, add the quartered red onion and crushed garlic, and sauté gently for 2–3 minutes. Add half the potatoes slices to the skillet, covering the base of the skillet.

4 Cover the potato slices with the carrot, broccoli, and bean curd. Sprinkle with half the sage and cover with the remaining potato slices. Sprinkle the grated cheese over the top.

5 Cook over a moderate heat for 8–10 minutes, then heat under a preheated broiler for 2–3 minutes, or until the cheese melts and browns.

6 Garnish with the remaining sage and serve straight from the skillet.

COOK'S TIP

Make sure that the mixture fills the whole width of your skillet so that all the layers remain intact.

Four Cheese & Potato Layer Bake

This is a quick dish to prepare and it can be left to cook in the oven without requiring any further attention. Vary the combination of hard cheeses and vegetables, according to what you have to hand.

Serves 4

INGREDIENTS

2 pounds unpeeled waxy potatoes, cut into wedges
2 tbsp butter
1 red onion, halved and sliced
2 garlic cloves, crushed
$1/4$ cup all-purpose flour
$2^{1}/2$ cups milk

14 ounce can artichoke hearts in brine, drained and halved
$5^{1}/2$ ounces frozen mixed vegetables, thawed
$1^{1}/8$ cup grated Swiss cheese
$1^{1}/8$ cup grated sharp cheese,

$1/2$ cup crumbled Gorgonzola cheese
$1/3$ cup grated Parmesan cheese
8 ounces bean curd, sliced
2 tbsp chopped fresh thyme
salt and pepper
thyme sprigs, to garnish

1 Cook the potato wedges in a saucepan of boiling water for 10 minutes. Drain thoroughly.

2 Meanwhile, melt the butter in a saucepan. Add the sliced onion and garlic and sauté gently for 2–3 minutes.

3 Stir the flour into the pan and cook for 1 minute. Gradually add the milk and bring to a boil, stirring constantly.

4 Reduce the heat and add the artichoke hearts, mixed vegetables, half of each of the 4 cheeses, and the bean curd to the pan, mixing well. Stir in the chopped fresh thyme and season with salt and pepper to taste.

5 Arrange a layer of parboiled potato wedges in the base of a shallow ovenproof dish. Spoon the vegetable mixture over the top and cover with the remaining potato wedges. Sprinkle the rest of the 4 cheeses over the top.

6 Cook in a preheated oven at 400°F for 30 minutes, or until the potatoes are cooked and the top is golden brown. Serve the bake garnished with fresh thyme sprigs.

Potato & Eggplant Gratin

Similar to a simple moussaka, *this recipe is made up of layers of eggplant, tomato, and potato baked with a yogurt topping.*

Serves 4

INGREDIENTS

1 pound waxy potatoes, sliced
1 tbsp vegetable oil
1 onion, chopped
2 garlic cloves, crushed
1 pound bean curd, diced

2 tbsp tomato paste
2 tbsp all-purpose flour
1¼ cups vegetable stock
2 large tomatoes, sliced

1 eggplant, sliced
2 tbsp chopped fresh thyme
1 pound unsweetened yogurt
2 eggs, beaten
salt and pepper

1 Cook the sliced potatoes in a saucepan of boiling water for 10 minutes, until tender but not breaking up. Drain and set aside.

2 Heat the oil in a pan and sauté the onion and garlic for 2–3 minutes.

3 Add the diced bean curd, tomato paste, and flour and cook for 1 minute. Gradually stir in the vegetable stock and bring to a boil, stirring constantly. Reduce the heat and simmer for 10 minutes.

4 Arrange a layer of the potato slices in the base of a deep ovenproof dish. Spoon the bean curd mixture on top.

5 Layer the tomatoes, then the eggplant, and then the remaining potato slices on top of the tofu mixture, making sure that it is completely covered.

6 Mix the yogurt and beaten eggs together in a bowl and season well with salt and pepper. Spoon the yogurt topping over the sliced potatoes.

7 Cook in a preheated oven at 375°F for 35–45 minutes, or until the topping is browned. Serve hot, with crisp salad greens.

VARIATION

You can use marinated or smoked bean curd for extra flavor, if you wish.

Spicy Potato & Nut Terrine

This delicious baked terrine has a base of mashed potato which is flavored with nuts, cheese, herbs, and spices.

Serves 4

INGREDIENTS

8 ounces mealy potatoes, diced
1¹/₂ cups pecans
1¹/₂ cups unsalted cashews
1 onion, chopped finely
2 garlic cloves, crushed
1¹/₂ cups diced open-cap
   mushrooms
2 tbsp butter

2 tbsp chopped mixed herbs
1 tsp paprika
1 tsp ground cumin
1 tsp ground coriander
4 eggs, beaten
4¹/₂ ounces full-fat soft cheese
²/₃ cup grated Parmesan cheese
salt and pepper

SAUCE:
3 large tomatoes, skinned, seeded,
   and chopped
2 tbsp tomato paste
¹/₃ cup red wine
1 tbsp red wine vinegar
pinch of superfine sugar

1 Lightly grease a 2-pound loaf pan and line with baking parchment.

2 Cook the potatoes in a pan of boiling water for 10 minutes, or until cooked through. Drain and mash the potatoes.

3 Finely chop the pecans and cashews or process in a food processor. Mix the nuts with the onion, garlic, and mushrooms. Melt the butter in a skillet and cook the nut mixture for 5–7 minutes. Add the herbs and spices to the pan. Stir in the eggs, cheeses, and potatoes and season.

4 Spoon the mixture into the prepared loaf pan, pressing down firmly. Cook in a preheated oven at 375°F, for 1 hour, or until set.

5 To make the sauce, mix the tomatoes, tomato paste, wine, wine vinegar, and sugar in a pan and bring to a boil, stirring. Cook for 10 minutes, or until the tomatoes have reduced. Pass the sauce through a strainer or blend in a food processor for 30 seconds. Turn the terrine out of the pan and cut into slices. Serve immediately with a little of the tomato sauce.

Pies & Bakes

The following chapter includes a range of hearty savory pies and bakes which are ideal for cold fall and winter evenings. However, a few less robust meals are also included which are more suitable for a light spring or summer meal. Many of the recipes are adaptable, and you may like to substitute your favorite vegetables for the ones suggested in the recipe, or vary them according to seasonal availability.

There are both sweet and savory recipes in this chapter, as the sweet potato lends itself to sweeter dishes, mixed with fruit and spices. Also included are a few bread recipes, as the potato makes excellent bread; an assortment of fabulous pies using different pastries; and pastry bites, such as turnovers. This chapter contains something for every occasion, illustrating how well the potato lends itself to a wide variety of dishes.

Potato, Beef, & Leek Turnovers

Filled with potatoes, cubes of beef, and leeks, these turnovers make a substantial meal. They are also perfect snacks for a picnic or barbecue.

Makes 4

INGREDIENTS

8 ounces waxy potatoes, diced
1 small carrot, diced
8 ounces beef steak, cubed

1 leek, sliced
8 ounces ready-made pie dough

1 tbsp butter
salt and pepper
1 egg, beaten

1 Lightly grease a cookie sheet with a little butter.

2 Mix the potatoes, carrots, beef, and leek in a large bowl. Season well with salt and pepper.

3 Divide the pie dough into 4 equal portions. On a lightly floured surface, roll each portion into an 8-inch round.

4 Spoon the potato mixture onto one half of each round, to within 1/2 inch of the edge. Top the potato mixture with the butter, dividing it equally between the 4 rounds. Brush the pie dough edge with a little of the beaten egg.

5 Fold the pie dough over to encase the filling and crimp the edges together.

6 Transfer the turnovers to the prepared cookie sheet and brush them with the remaining beaten egg.

7 Cook in a preheated oven at 400°F for 20 minutes. Reduce the oven temperature to 325°F and cook the turnovers for a further 30 minutes until cooked and golden brown.

8 Serve the pasties with a crisp salad or onion gravy.

COOK'S TIP

These turnovers can be made in advance and frozen.

VARIATION

Use other types of meat, such as pork or chicken, in the turnovers and add chunks of apple in step 2, if desired.

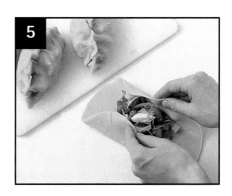

Potato & Tomato Calzone

*These pizza dough Italian turnovers are best served hot
with a salad as a delicious lunch or supper dish.*

Makes 4

INGREDIENTS

DOUGH:
4 cups white bread flour
1 tsp active dry yeast
1 1/4 cups vegetable stock
1 tbsp clear honey
1 tsp caraway seeds
milk, for glazing

FILLING:
8 ounces waxy potatoes, diced
1 tbsp vegetable oil
1 onion, halved and sliced
2 garlic cloves, crushed
2/3 cup sun-dried tomatoes
2 tbsp chopped fresh basil

2 tbsp tomato paste
2 celery stalks, sliced
1/2 cup grated mozzarella cheese

1 To make the dough, sift the flour into a large mixing bowl and stir in the yeast. Make a well in the center of the mixture.

2 Stir in the vegetable stock, honey, and caraway seeds and bring the mixture together to form a dough.

3 Turn the dough out onto a lightly floured surface and knead for 8 minutes, until smooth. Place the dough in a lightly oiled mixing bowl, cover, and leave to rise in a warm place for 1 hour, or until it has doubled in size.

4 Meanwhile, make the filling. Heat the oil in a skillet and add all the remaining ingredients, except for the cheese. Cook for about 5 minutes, stirring.

5 Divide the risen dough into 4 pieces. On a lightly floured surface, roll them out to form 7-inch rounds. Spoon equal amounts of the filling onto one half of each circle.

6 Sprinkle the cheese over the filling. Brush the edge of the dough with milk and fold the dough over to form 4 semicircles, pressing to seal the edges.

7 Place on a nonstick cookie sheet and brush with milk. Cook in a preheated oven at 425°F for 30 minutes, until golden.

Potato & Meat Filo Packets

These small packets are perfect for special occasions when you want to impress your guests. Crisp pastry encases a tasty potato and beef filling which is cooked in red wine for a delicious flavor.

Serves 4

INGREDIENTS

8 ounces waxy potatoes, finely diced
1 tbsp vegetable oil
4¹/₂ ounces ground beef
1 leek, sliced
1 small yellow bell pepper, finely
  diced
2 cups sliced button mushrooms

1 tbsp all-purpose flour
1 tbsp tomato paste
¹/₃ cup red wine
¹/₃ cup beef stock
1 tbsp chopped fresh rosemary
8 ounces filo pastry, thawed
  if frozen

2 tbsp butter, melted
salt and pepper

1 Cook the diced potatoes in a saucepan of boiling water for 5 minutes. Drain and set aside.

2 Meanwhile, heat the oil in a saucepan and sauté the ground beef, leek, yellow bell pepper, and mushrooms over a low heat for 5 minutes.

3 Stir in the flour and tomato paste and cook for 1 minute. Gradually add the red wine and beef stock, stirring to thicken. Add the rosemary, season to taste with salt and pepper, and let cool slightly.

4 Lay 4 sheets of filo pastry on a counter or board. Brush each sheet with butter and lay a second layer of filo on top. Trim the sheets to make four 8-inch squares.

5 Brush the edges of the pastry with a little butter. Spoon a quarter of the beef mixture into the center of each square. Bring up the corners and the sides of the squares to form a packet, scrunching the edges together. Make sure that the packets are well sealed by pressing the pastry together, otherwise the filling will leak during baking.

6 Place the packets on a cookie sheet and brush with butter. Bake in a preheated oven at 350°F for 20 minutes. Serve hot.

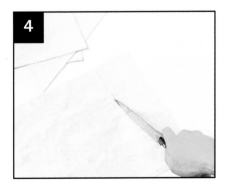

Carrot-topped Beef Pie

This is a variation of an old favorite, where creamy mashed potato is piled thickly onto a delicious beef pie filling. Here the potato is given extra flavor and color by the addition of carrots and herbs.

Serves 4

INGREDIENTS

1 pound ground beef
1 onion, chopped
1 garlic clove, crushed
1 tbsp all-purpose flour
1 1/4 cups beef stock

2 tbsp tomato paste
1 celery stalk, chopped
3 tbsp chopped fresh parsley
1 tbsp Worcestershire sauce
1 1/2 pounds mealy potatoes, diced
2 large carrots, diced

2 tbsp butter
3 tbsp milk
salt and pepper

1 Dry-fry the beef in a large pan set over a high heat for 3–4 minutes, or until sealed. Add the onion and garlic and cook for a further 5 minutes, stirring.

2 Add the flour and cook for 1 minute. Gradually blend in the beef stock and tomato paste. Stir in the celery, 1 tbsp of the parsley, and the Worcestershire sauce. Season to taste with salt and pepper.

3 Bring the mixture to a boil, then reduce the heat, and simmer for 20–25 minutes. Spoon the beef mixture into a 5-cup pie dish.

4 Meanwhile, cook the potatoes and carrots in a saucepan of boiling water for 10 minutes. Drain and mash them together.

5 Stir the butter, milk, and the remaining parsley into the potato and carrot mixture and season. Spoon the potato on top of the beef mixture to cover it completely; alternatively, pipe the potato with a pastry bag.

6 Cook the pie in a preheated oven at 375°F for 45 minutes, or until cooked through and piping hot. Serve immediately.

VARIATION

You can use ground lamb, turkey, or pork instead of the beef, adding appropriate herbs, such as rosemary and sage, for added flavor.

Potato, Beef, & Kidney Pie

Steak and kidney has always been a popular pie filling, but this version is particularly good as it is cooked in a beer sauce with added chunks of potato.

Serves 4

INGREDIENTS

8 ounces waxy potatoes, cubed
2 tbsp butter
1 pound lean steak, cubed
5$\frac{1}{2}$ ounces ox kidney, cored
  and chopped

12 shallots
$\frac{1}{4}$ cup all-purpose flour
$\frac{2}{3}$ cup beef stock
$\frac{2}{3}$ cup strong, dark beer

8 ounces ready-made puff pastry
1 egg, beaten
salt and pepper

1 Cook the cubed potatoes in a saucepan of boiling water for 10 minutes. Drain thoroughly.

2 Meanwhile, melt the butter in a saucepan and add the steak cubes and the kidney. Cook for 5 minutes, stirring, until the meat is sealed on all sides.

3 Add the shallots and cook for a further 3–4 minutes. Stir in the flour and cook for 1 minute. Gradually stir in the beef stock and beer and bring to a boil, stirring constantly.

4 Stir the potatoes into the meat mixture and season with salt and pepper. Reduce the heat until the mixture is simmering. Cover the saucepan and cook for 1 hour, stirring occasionally.

5 Spoon the beef mixture into the base of a pie dish. Roll the pastry on a lightly floured surface until $\frac{1}{2}$ inch larger than the top of the dish.

6 Cut a strip of pastry long enough and wide enough to fit around the edge of the dish.

Brush the edge of the dish with beaten egg and press the pastry strip around the edge. Brush with egg and place the pastry lid on top. Crimp to seal the edge and brush with beaten egg.

7 Cook in a preheated oven at 450°F for 20–25 minutes, or until the pastry has risen and is golden. Serve hot, straight from the dish.

Raised Potato, Pork, & Apple Pie

The pastry used in this recipe requires fairly speedy working, as it is molded into the pan while it is warm and pliable. It is very easy to make and results in a fabulous crisp pastry.

Serves 8

INGREDIENTS

FILLING:
2 pounds waxy potatoes, sliced
2 tbsp butter
2 tbsp vegetable oil
1 pound lean pork, cubed
2 onions, sliced
4 garlic cloves, crushed
4 tbsp tomato paste

2 1/2 cups stock
2 tbsp chopped fresh sage
2 eating apples, peeled and sliced
salt and pepper

PASTRY:
6 cups all-purpose flour
pinch of salt

10 tsp butter
1/2 cup shortening
1 1/4 cups water
1 egg, beaten
1 tsp gelatin

1 Cook the potatoes in boiling water for 10 minutes. Drain and set aside. Heat the butter and oil in a flameproof casserole dish and fry the pork until browned, turning. Add the onion and garlic and cook for 5 minutes. Stir in the rest of the filling ingredients, except for the potatoes and the apples. Reduce the heat, cover, and simmer for 1 1/2 hours. Drain the stock from the casserole dish and reserve. Let the pork cool.

2 To make the pastry, sift the flour into a bowl. Add the salt and make a well in the center. Melt the butter and shortening in a pan with the water; then bring to a boil. Pour into the flour and mix to form a dough. Turn the dough out onto a floured surface and knead until smooth. Reserve a quarter of the dough and use the rest to line the base and sides of a large pie pan or deep 8-inch loose-bottom cake pan.

3 Layer the pork, potatoes, and the apple in the base. Roll out the reserved pastry to make a lid. Dampen the edges and place the lid on top, sealing well. Brush with egg and make a hole in the top. Cook in a preheated oven at 400°F for 30 minutes, then at 325°F for 45 minutes. Dissolve the gelatin in the reserved stock and pour into the hole in the lid as the pie cools. Cool and chill. Serve the pie with a salad.

Potato, Sausage, & Onion Pie

This is a delicious supper dish for all the family.
Use good quality herb sausages for a really tasty pie.

Serves 4

INGREDIENTS

2 large waxy potatoes, unpeeled and
    sliced
2 tbsp butter
4 thick pork and herb sausages
1 leek, sliced

2 garlic cloves, crushed
$2/3$ cup vegetable stock
$1^2/3$ cup hard cider or apple juice
2 tbsp chopped fresh sage
2 tbsp cornstarch

4 tbsp water
$3/4$ cup grated sharp cheese
salt and pepper

1 Cook the sliced potatoes in a saucepan of boiling water for 10 minutes. Drain and set aside.

2 Meanwhile, melt the butter in a skillet and cook the sausages for 8–10 minutes, turning them frequently so that they brown on all sides. Remove the sausages from the skillet and cut them into thick slices.

3 Add the leek, garlic, and sausage slices to the skillet and cook for 2–3 minutes.

4 Add the vegetable stock, cider or apple juice, and chopped sage. Season with salt and pepper. Blend the cornstarch with the water. Stir it into the skillet and bring to a boil, stirring until the sauce is thick and clear. Spoon the mixture into the base of a deep pie dish.

5 Layer the potato slices on top of the sausage mixture to cover it completely. Season with salt and pepper and sprinkle the grated cheese over the top.

6 Cook in a preheated oven at 375°F for 25–30 minutes, or until the potatoes are cooked and the cheese is golden brown. Serve the pie hot.

VARIATION

Other vegetables, such as broccoli or cauliflower, can be added to the filling. You can use white wine instead of the cider or apple juice, if you prefer.

Potato & Broccoli Pie

The sauce for this pie is flavored with rich dolcelatte cheese and walnuts, which are delicious with broccoli. Make either one large pie or 4 individual pies and serve with fresh vegetables.

Serves 4

INGREDIENTS

1 pound waxy potatoes, cut into
  chunks
2 tbsp butter
1 tbsp vegetable oil
6 ounces lean pork, cubed
1 red onion, cut into 8

$^1/_4$ cup all-purpose flour
$^2/_3$ cup vegetable stock
$^2/_3$ cup milk
$^3/_4$ cup crumbled dolcelatte or other
  creamy blue cheese
6 ounces broccoli flowerets

3 tbsp walnuts
8 ounces ready-made puff pastry
milk, for glazing
salt and pepper

1 Cook the potato chunks in a saucepan of boiling water for 5 minutes. Drain and set aside.

2 Meanwhile, heat the butter and oil in a heavy-based pan. Add the pork cubes and cook for 5 minutes, turning until browned.

3 Add the onion and cook for a further 2 minutes. Stir in the flour and cook for 1 minute, then gradually stir in the vegetable stock and milk. Bring to a boil, stirring constantly.

4 Add the cheese, broccoli, potatoes, and walnuts to the pan and simmer for 5 minutes. Season with salt and pepper to taste, then spoon the mixture into a pie dish.

5 On a floured surface, roll out the pastry until 1 inch larger than the dish. Cut a 1-inch wide strip from the pastry . Dampen the edge of the dish and place the pastry strip around it. Brush the strip with milk and put the pastry lid on top.

6 Seal and crimp the edges and make 2 small slits in the center of the lid. Brush with milk to glaze and cook in a preheated oven at 400°F for 25 minutes, or until the pastry has risen and is golden.

COOK'S TIP

Use a hard cheese such as sharp cheese instead of the dolcelatte, if you prefer.

Potato & Ham Pie

This pie contains chunks of pineapple—a classic accompaniment to ham—with potatoes and onion in a mustard sauce, all encased in a crumbly cheese-flavored pastry.

Serves 4

INGREDIENTS

8 ounces waxy potatoes, cubed
2 tbsp butter
8 shallots, halved
1¹⁄₃ cups diced smoked ham
¹⁄₄ cup all-purpose flour
1¹⁄₄ cups milk
2 tbsp wholegrain mustard

1³⁄₄ ounces pineapple, cubed

PASTRY:
2 cups all-purpose flour
¹⁄₂ tsp dry mustard
pinch of salt
pinch of cayenne pepper

²⁄₃ cup butter
1 cup grated sharp cheese
2 egg yolks, plus extra for brushing
4–6 tsp cold water

1 Cook the potato cubes in a saucepan of boiling water for 10 minutes. Drain and set aside.

2 Meanwhile, melt the butter in a pan, add the shallots, and sauté for 3–4 minutes, until they begin to color.

3 Add the ham and cook for 2–3 minutes. Stir in the flour and cook for 1 minute. Gradually stir in the milk. Add the mustard and pineapple and bring to a boil, stirring. Season well with salt and pepper and add the potatoes.

4 Sift the flour for the pastry into a bowl with the mustard, salt, and cayenne. Rub the butter into the mixture until it resembles bread crumbs. Add the cheese and mix to form a dough with the egg yolks and water.

5 On a floured surface, roll out half the pastry and line a shallow pie dish. Trim the edges.

6 Spoon the filling into the pie dish. Brush the edges of the pastry with water.

7 Roll out the remaining pastry to make a lid and press it on top of the pie, sealing the edges. Decorate the top of the pie with the pastry trimmings. Brush the pie with egg yolk and cook in a preheated oven at 375°F for 40–45 minutes, or until the pastry is cooked and golden.

Potato & Turkey Pie

Turkey is especially good with fruit, as it has a fairly strong flavor, more so if the dark meat is used. The walnuts counteract the sweetness of the fruit, adding crunch and a slightly bitter flavor.

Serves 4

INGREDIENTS

10 1/2 ounces waxy potatoes, diced
2 tbsp butter
1 tbsp vegetable oil
10 1/2 ounces lean turkey meat, cubed
1 red onion, halved and sliced

1/4 cup all-purpose flour
1 1/4 cups milk
2/3 cup heavy cream
2 celery stalks, sliced
1/3 cup dried apricots, chopped

3 tbsp walnut pieces
2 tbsp chopped fresh parsley
salt and pepper
8 ounces ready made pie dough
beaten egg, for brushing

1 Cook the diced potatoes in a saucepan of boiling water for 10 minutes, until tender. Drain and set aside.

2 Meanwhile, heat the butter and oil in a saucepan. Add the turkey and cook for 5 minutes, turning until browned.

3 Add the sliced onion and cook for 2–3 minutes. Stir in the flour and cook for 1 minute. Gradually stir in the milk and the heavy cream. Bring to a boil, stirring, then reduce the heat until the mixture is simmering.

4 Stir in the celery, apricots, walnut pieces, parsley, and potatoes. Season well with salt and pepper. Spoon the potato and turkey mixture into the base of a 5-cup pie dish.

5 On a lightly floured surface, roll out the pie dough until it is 1 inch larger than the dish. Trim a 1-inch wide strip from the pie dough and place the strip on the dampened rim of the dish. Brush the strip with water and cover with the pie dough lid, pressing to seal the edges.

6 Brush the top of the pie with beaten egg to glaze and cook in a preheated oven at 400°F for 25–30 minutes, or until the pie dough is cooked and golden brown. Serve at once.

Potato Crisp Pie

This is a layered pie of potatoes, broccoli, tomatoes, and chicken slices in a creamy sauce, topped with a crisp oaty layer. Use strips of beef or pork for an equally delicious dish, if desired.

Serves 4

INGREDIENTS

2 large waxy potatoes, sliced
1/4 cup butter
1 skinless chicken breast fillet, about
   6 oz
2 garlic cloves, crushed
4 scallions, sliced

1/4 cup all-purpose flour
2/3 cup dry white wine
2/3 cup heavy cream
8 ounces broccoli flowerets
4 large tomatoes, sliced
3 ounces Swiss cheese, sliced

1 cup unsweetened yogurt
1/3 cup rolled oats, toasted

1 Cook the potatoes in a saucepan of boiling water for 10 minutes. Drain and set aside.

2 Meanwhile, melt the butter in a skillet. Cut the chicken into strips and cook for 5 minutes, turning. Add the garlic and scallions and cook for a further 2 minutes.

3 Stir in the flour and cook for 1 minute. Gradually add the wine and cream. Bring to a boil, stirring, then reduce the heat until the sauce is simmering, then cook for 5 minutes.

4 Meanwhile, blanch the broccoli in boiling water, drain, and rinse in cold water.

5 Place half the potatoes in the base of a pie dish and top with half the tomatoes and half the broccoli.

6 Spoon the chicken sauce on top and repeat the layers in the same order once more.

7 Arrange the slices of Swiss cheese on top and spoon over the yogurt. Sprinkle with the oats and cook in a preheated oven at 400°F for 25 minutes, until the top is golden brown. Serve the pie immediately.

COOK'S TIP

Add chopped nuts, such as pine nuts, to the topping for extra crunch, if desired.

Potato, Leek, & Chicken Pie

This pie has an attractive filo pie shell which has a "ruffled" top made with strips of the pastry brushed with melted butter.

Serves 4

INGREDIENTS

8 ounces waxy potatoes, cubed
¼ cup butter
1 skinless chicken breast fillet, about 6 oz, cubed
1 leek, sliced

2½ cups sliced crimini or champignon marron mushrooms
¼ cup all-purpose flour
1¼ cups milk
1 tbsp Dijon mustard

2 tbsp chopped fresh sage
8 ounces filo pastry, thawed if frozen
3 tbsp butter, melted
salt and pepper

1 Cook the potato cubes in a saucepan of boiling water for 5 minutes. Drain and set aside.

2 Melt the butter in a skillet and cook the chicken cubes for 5 minutes, or until browned all over.

3 Add the leek and mushrooms and cook for 3 minutes, stirring. Stir in the flour and cook for 1 minute. Gradually add the milk and bring to a boil. Add the mustard, chopped sage, and potato cubes, lower the heat, and simmer for 10 minutes.

4 Meanwhile, line a deep pie dish with half of the sheets of filo pastry. Spoon the sauce into the dish and cover with one sheet of pastry. Brush the pastry with butter and lay another sheet on top. Brush this sheet with butter.

5 Cut the remaining filo pastry into strips and fold them on to the top of the pie to create a ruffled effect. Brush the strips with the melted butter and cook in a preheated oven 350°F for 45 minutes, or until golden brown and crisp. Serve hot.

COOK'S TIP

If the top of the pie starts to brown too quickly, cover it with foil halfway through the cooking time, to allow the pastry base to cook through without the top burning.

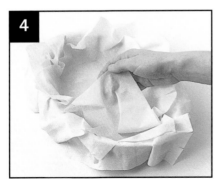

Layered Fish & Potato Pie

This is a really delicious and filling dish. Layers of potato slices and mixed fish are cooked in a creamy sauce and topped with grated cheese.

Serves 4

INGREDIENTS

2 pounds waxy potatoes, sliced
1/4 cup butter
1 red onion, halved and sliced
1/3 cup all-purpose flour
2 cups milk

2/3 cup heavy cream
8 ounces smoked haddock fillet, cubed
8 ounces cod fillet, cubed

1 red bell pepper, diced
4 1/2 ounces broccoli flowerets
2/3 cup grated Parmesan cheese
salt and pepper

1 Cook the sliced potatoes in a saucepan of boiling water for 10 minutes. Drain and set aside.

2 Meanwhile, melt the butter in a saucepan, add the onion and sauté gently for 3–4 minutes.

3 Add the flour and cook for 1 minute. Blend in the milk and cream and bring to a boil, stirring until thickened.

4 Arrange half the potato slices in the base of a shallow ovenproof dish.

5 Add the fish, diced bell pepper, and broccoli to the sauce and cook over a low heat for 10 minutes. Season with salt and pepper, then spoon the mixture on top of the potatoes in the dish.

6 Arrange the remaining potato slices in a layer on the fish mixture. Sprinkle the Parmesan cheese over the top.

7 Cook in a preheated oven at 350°F for 30 minutes, or until the potatoes are cooked and the top is golden.

COOK'S TIP

Choose your favorite combination of fish, adding salmon or various shellfish for special occasions.

Potato-topped Smoked Fish Pie

This fish pie has a tasty filling hidden beneath a creamy potato and rutabaga topping flavored with fresh herbs, making it appealing to both the eye and taste buds.

Serves 4

INGREDIENTS

1 pound mealy potatoes, diced
8 ounces rutabaga, diced
1/4 cup butter
1 leek, sliced
1 3/4 ounces baby corn cobs, sliced
1 zucchini, halved and sliced
1/3 cup all-purpose flour

1 1/4 cups milk
2/3 cup fish stock
2/3 cup heavy cream
1 pound smoked cod fillet, cut into cubes
few drops of Tabasco sauce
4 1/2 ounces cooked peeled shrimp

2 tbsp chopped fresh parsley
2 tbsp grated Parmesan cheese
salt and pepper

1 Cook the potatoes and rutabaga in a saucepan of boiling water for 20 minutes, until very tender. Drain and mash thoroughly until smooth.

2 Meanwhile, melt the butter in a saucepan, add the leeks, corn cobs, and zucchini and sauté gently for 3–4 minutes, stirring.

3 Add the flour and cook for 1 minute. Gradually blend in the milk, fish stock, and cream and bring to a boil, stirring until the mixture begins to thicken.

4 Stir in the fish, reduce the heat, and cook for 5 minutes. Add the Tabasco sauce, shrimp, and half the parsley, and season. Spoon the mixture into the base of an ovenproof dish.

5 Mix the remaining parsley into the potato and rutabaga mixture, season, and spoon or pipe onto the fish mixture, covering it completely. Sprinkle with the grated cheese and cook in a preheated oven at 350°F for 20 minutes, until cooked through. Serve the pie immediately.

VARIATION

Add cooked mashed parsnip to the potato instead of the rutabaga.

Potato, Tuna, & Cheese Quiche

The base for this quiche is made from mashed potato instead of pastry,
giving a softer textured shell for the tasty tuna filling.

Serves 4

INGREDIENTS

1 pound mealy potatoes, diced
2 tbsp butter
6 tbsp all-purpose flour

FILLING:
1 tbsp vegetable oil
1 shallot, chopped
1 garlic clove, crushed

1 red bell pepper, diced
6 ounce can tuna in brine, drained
$^1/_3$ cup canned corn, drained
$^2/_3$ cup milk
3 eggs, beaten
1 tbsp chopped fresh dill
$^1/_3$ cup grated sharp cheese
salt and pepper

TO GARNISH:
fresh dill sprigs
lemon wedges

1 Cook the potatoes in a pan of boiling water for 10 minutes, or until tender. Drain and mash the potatoes. Add the butter and flour and mix to form a dough.

2 Knead the potato dough on a floured surface and press the mixture into an 8-inch quiche pan. Prick the base with a fork. Line with baking parchment and dried beans and bake in a preheated oven at 400°F for 20 minutes.

3 Heat the oil in a skillet, add the onion, garlic, and bell pepper, and sauté gently for 5 minutes. Drain well and spoon into the flan shell. Flake the tuna and arrange it over the top.

4 In a bowl, mix the milk, eggs, and chopped dill together. Season with salt and pepper.

5 Pour the egg and dill mixture into the flan shell and sprinkle the grated cheese on top.

6 Bake in the oven for 20 minutes, or until the filling has set. Garnish the quiche with fresh dill and lemon wedges. Serve with mixed vegetables or salad.

VARIATION

Use any other cooked fish of your choice, or canned crab meat instead of the tuna, if desired.

Potato-topped Lentil Bake

This is a great dish for vegetarians and meat-eaters alike. A delicious mixture of red lentils, bean curd, and vegetables is cooked beneath a crunchy potato topping for a really hearty meal.

Serves 4

INGREDIENTS

TOPPING:
1¹/₂ pounds mealy potatoes, diced
2 tbsp butter
1 tbsp milk
¹/₂ cup chopped pecans
2 tbsp chopped fresh thyme
thyme sprigs, to garnish

FILLING:
1 cup red lentils
¹/₄ cup butter
1 leek, sliced
2 garlic cloves, crushed
1 celery stalk, chopped
4¹/₂ ounces broccoli flowerets

6 ounces smoked bean curd, cubed
2 tsp tomato paste
salt and pepper

1 To make the topping, cook the potatoes in a saucepan of boiling water for 10–15 minutes, or until tender. Drain well, add the butter and milk, and mash thoroughly. Stir in the pecans and chopped thyme and set aside.

2 Cook the lentils in boiling water for 20–30 minutes, or until tender. Drain and set aside.

3 Melt the butter in a pan, add the leek, garlic, celery, and broccoli. Cook for 5 minutes, then add the bean curd cubes.

4 Stir the lentils into the bean curd and vegetable mixture together with the tomato paste. Season with salt and pepper to taste, then turn the mixture into the base of a shallow ovenproof dish.

5 Spoon the mashed potato on top of the lentil mixture to cover it completely.

6 Cook in a preheated oven at 400°F for 30–35 minutes, or until the topping is golden. Garnish with sprigs of fresh thyme and serve hot.

VARIATION

You can use any combination of vegetables in this dish. You can also add sliced cooked meat instead of the cubed bean curd for a nonvegetarian dish.

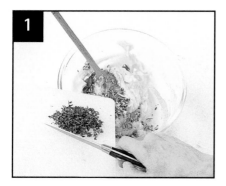

Potato & Eggplant Layer

*These individual pies of layered potato, eggplant, and zucchini baked
in a tomato sauce can be made in advance and chilled for 24 hours before cooking.*

Serves 4

INGREDIENTS

3 large waxy potatoes, sliced thinly
1 small eggplant, sliced thinly
1 zucchini, sliced
2 tbsp vegetable oil
1 onion, diced
1 green bell pepper, diced

1 tsp cumin seeds
7 ounce can chopped tomatoes
2 tbsp chopped fresh basil
6 ounces mozarella cheese, sliced
8 ounces bean curd, sliced
1 cup fresh white bread crumbs

2 tbsp grated Parmesan cheese
salt and pepper
fresh basil leaves, to garnish

1 Cook the sliced potatoes in a saucepan of boiling water for 5 minutes. Drain and set aside.

2 Lay the eggplant slices on a plate, sprinkle with salt, and leave for 20 minutes. Blanch the zucchini in boiling water for 2–3 minutes. Drain and set aside.

3 Meanwhile, heat 2 tbsp of the oil in a skillet, add the onion, and sauté gently for 2–3 minutes, until softened. Add the bell pepper, cumin seeds, basil, and canned tomatoes. Season with salt and pepper. Reduce the heat and simmer for 30 minutes.

4 Rinse the eggplant slices and pat dry. Heat the remaining oil in a large skillet and fry the eggplant slices for 3–5 minutes, turning to brown both sides. Drain and set aside.

5 Arrange half the potato slices in the base of 4 small loose-bottomed flan pans. Cover with half the zucchini slices, half the eggplant slices, and half the mozzarella slices. Lay the bean curd on top and spoon over the tomato sauce. Repeat the layers of potatoes, zucchini, eggplant, and mozzarella cheese.

6 Mix the bread crumbs and Parmesan cheese together and sprinkle over the top. Cook in a preheated oven at 375°F for 25–30 minutes, or until golden. Garnish with basil leaves and serve immediately.

Sweet Potato Bread

This is a great tasting loaf, colored light orange by the sweet potato. Added sweetness from the honey is offset by the tangy orange rind and cinnamon.

Makes 1 loaf

INGREDIENTS

8 ounces sweet potatoes, diced
2/3 cup tepid water
2 tbsp clear honey
2 tbsp vegetable oil

3 tbsp orange juice
1/2 cup semolina
2 cups white bread flour
1 packet active dry yeast

1 tsp ground cinnamon
grated rind of 1 orange
1 cup butter

1 Lightly grease a 1½-pound loaf pan.

2 Cook the sweet potatoes in a saucepan of boiling water for 10 minutes, or until soft. Drain well and mash until smooth.

3 Meanwhile, mix the water, honey, oil, and orange juice together in a large mixing bowl.

4 Add the mashed sweet potatoes, semolina, three-quarters of the flour, the yeast, cinnamon, and orange rind and mix well to form a dough. Let stand for about 10 minutes.

5 Cut the butter into small pieces and knead it into the dough with the remaining flour. Knead for about 5 minutes, until the dough is smooth.

6 Place the dough in the prepared loaf pan. Cover and leave in a warm place to rise for 1 hour or until doubled in size.

7 Cook the loaf in a preheated oven at 375°F for 45–60 minutes, or until the base sounds hollow when tapped with the knuckles. Serve the bread warm, cut into slices.

COOK'S TIP

If the baked loaf does not sound hollow on the base when it is tapped, remove it from the pan and return it to the oven for a few extra minutes, until thoroughly cooked.

Cheese & Potato Braid

This bread has a delicious cheese and garlic flavor, and is best eaten straight from the oven.

Makes one 1 pound loaf

INGREDIENTS

6 ounces mealy potatoes, diced
2 packets active dry yeast
6 cups white bread flour

2 cups vegetable stock
2 garlic cloves, crushed
2 tbsp chopped fresh rosemary

1 cup grated Swiss cheese
1 tbsp vegetable oil
1 tbsp salt

1 Lightly grease and flour a cookie sheet.

2 Cook the potatoes in a pan of boiling water for 10 minutes, or until soft. Drain and mash.

3 Transfer the mashed potatoes to a large mixing bowl, stir in the yeast, flour, and stock and mix to form a smooth dough.

4 Add the garlic, rosemary, and $^3/_4$ cup of the cheese and knead the dough for 5 minutes. Make a hollow in the dough, pour in the oil, and knead the dough.

5 Cover the dough and leave it to rise in a warm place for $1^1/_2$ hours, or until doubled in size.

6 Knead the dough again and divide it into 3 equal portions. Roll each portion into a 14-inch sausage shape.

7 Pressing one end of each of the sausage shapes together, braid the dough and fold the remaining ends under.

8 Place the braid on the cookie sheet, cover, and leave to rise for 30 minutes.

9 Sprinkle the remaining cheese over the top of the braid and cook in a preheated oven at 375°F for 40 minutes, or until the base of the loaf sounds hollow when tapped. Cool slightly, then serve warm.

VARIATION

Instead of making a braid, use the mixture to make a batch of cheese-flavored rolls, which would be ideal to serve with hot soup.

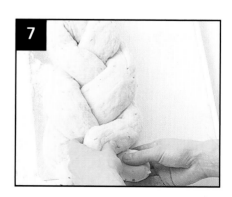

Potato & Nutmeg Scones

Making these scones with mashed potato gives them a slightly different texture from traditional scones, but they are just as delicious served warm and spread with butter.

Makes 8

INGREDIENTS

8 ounces mealy potatoes, diced
1 cup all-purpose flour
1$^1/_2$ tsp baking powder

$^1/_2$ tsp grated nutmeg
$^1/_3$ cup golden raisins
1 egg, beaten

$^1/_4$ cup heavy cream
2 tsp light brown sugar

1 Line and grease a cookie sheet.

2 Cook the diced potatoes in a saucepan of boiling water for 10 minutes, or until soft. Drain well and mash the potatoes.

3 Transfer the mashed potatoes to a large mixing bowl and stir in the flour, baking powder, and nutmeg.

4 Stir in the golden raisins, egg, and cream and beat the mixture with a spoon until smooth.

5 Shape the mixture into 8 rounds $^3/_4$ inch thick and put on the cookie sheet.

6 Cook in a preheated oven at 400°F for about 15 minutes, or until the scones have risen and are golden. Sprinkle the scones with sugar and serve warm and spread with butter.

VARIATION

This recipe may be used to make one large scone "cake" instead of the 8 small scones, if desired.

COOK'S TIP

For extra convenience, make a batch of scones in advance and open-freeze them. Thaw thoroughly and warm in a moderate oven when ready to serve.

Potato Muffins

These light-textured muffins rise like little soufflés in the oven and are best eaten warm straight from the oven. The dried fruits can be varied according to what you have to hand.

Serves 12

INGREDIENTS

6 ounces mealy potatoes, diced
³/4 cup self-rising flour

2 tbsp light brown sugar
1 tsp baking powder

³/4 cup raisins
4 eggs, separated

1 Lightly grease and flour 12 muffin pans.

2 Cook the diced potatoes in a saucepan of boiling water for 10 minutes, until cooked. Drain well and mash until smooth.

3 Transfer the mashed potatoes to a mixing bowl and add the flour, sugar, baking powder, raisins, and egg yolks. Stir well to mix thoroughly.

4 In a clean bowl, beat the egg whites until standing in peaks. Using a metal spoon, gently fold them into the potato mixture until fully incorporated.

5 Divide the mixture between the prepared pans.

6 Cook in a preheated oven at 400°F for 10 minutes. Reduce the oven temperature to 325°F and cook the muffins for 7–10 minutes, or until risen.

7 Remove the muffins from the pans and serve warm.

VARIATION

Other flavorings, such as cinnamon or nutmeg, can be added to the mixture, if desired.

COOK'S TIP

Instead of spreading the muffins with plain butter, serve them with cinnamon butter made by blending ¹/2 cup butter with a large pinch of ground cinnamon.

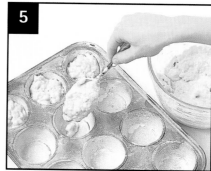

Fruity Potato Cake

Sweet potatoes mix beautifully with fruit and brown sugar for this delicious cake.
It makes a lovely dessert served with cream garnished with grated orange rind.

Makes one 7-inch cake

INGREDIENTS

1¹⁄₂ pounds sweet potatoes, diced
1 tbsp butter, melted
³⁄₄ ounces raw brown crystal sugar
3 eggs

3 tbsp milk
1 tbsp lemon juice
grated rind of 1 lemon
1 tsp caraway seeds

9 cups chopped dried fruits, such as
   apple, pear, or mango
2 tsp baking powder

1 Lightly grease a 7-inch square cake pan.

2 Cook the sweet potatoes in boiling water for 10 minutes, or until soft. Drain and mash the sweet potatoes until smooth.

3 Transfer the mashed sweet potatoes to a mixing bowl while still hot and add the butter and sugar, mixing to dissolve.

4 Beat in the eggs, lemon juice and rind, caraway seeds, and chopped dried fruit. Add the baking powder and mix well.

5 Pour the mixture into the prepared cake pan.

6 Cook in a preheated oven at 325°F for 1–1¹⁄₄ hours or until cooked through. Remove the cake from the pan and transfer to a wire rack to cool. Cut into thick slices to serve.

VARIATION

Add a few drops of rum or brandy to the mixture with the eggs and lemon juice in step 4, if desired.

COOK'S TIP

This cake is ideal as a special occasion dessert. It can be made in advance and frozen until required. Wrap the cake in plastic wrap and freeze. Thaw at room temperature for 24 hours and warm through in a moderate oven before serving.

Index

Index compiled by Hilary Bird.